CW01500491

MARX200

THE SIGNIFICANCE OF MARXISM
IN THE 21ST CENTURY

www.marx-memorial-library.org.uk

MARX200
THE SIGNIFICANCE OF MARXISM
IN THE 21ST CENTURY

ISBN: 978-1-899155-09-5

Published by Praxis Press, 2019.
Email: praxispress@me.com

Distributor: Unity Books, 72 Waterloo Street, Glasgow, G2 7DA,
Scotland, Great Britain
T: +44 141 204 1611
E: enquiries@unitybooks.co.uk
www.unitybooks.co.uk
www.facebook.com/unitybooksonline/

Copyright ©2019 Marx Memorial Library
All rights reserved. No part of this publication may be reproduced, distributed,
or transmitted in any form or by any means, including photocopying, recording,
or other electronic or mechanical methods, without the prior written permission of Marx Memorial Library, except in the case of brief quotations embodied
in critical reviews and certain other non-commercial uses permitted by copyright law.

Cover illustration: Junior Lopes (Brazil)

CONTENTS

Introduction

Marx200 – The Significance of Marxism in the 21ˢᵗ Century

This book is an edited selection of the contributions delivered at an international conference to mark the bicentenary of the birth of Karl Marx. However, both the conference and this, its outcome, were not conceived as purely celebratory events. The intention of Marx Memorial Library (MML) – the conference initiator and organiser – was to explore two important and related questions: is Marxism a living theory which enables us to understand social reality, and which, as a practice, helps to change our world?

This book is a modest attempt to throw some light on these two related questions. So, although our starting point is to revisit Marxist theory, we recognise that this is not enough. The challenge is to develop and apply this theory to the changed conditions of the 21ˢᵗ century.

Marx's conception of history, economics, politics and philosophy led to a penetrating analysis of historical change – the interaction between modes of production, relations of production and the consequent class struggle which generates such change. This was succinctly expressed by Engels in his oration at Marx's graveside in 1883:

> 'Just as Darwin discovered the law of development of organic nature, so Marx discovered the law of development of human history: the simple fact, hitherto concealed by an overgrowth of ideology, that mankind must first of all eat, drink, have shelter and clothing, before it can pursue politics, science, art, religion, etc.'[1]

In other words, social being determines consciousness. Social being is shaped by social production and this in turn means that humankind enters into:

> 'definite relations that are indispensable and independent of their will; these relations of production correspond to a definite stage of development of their material forces of production'.[2]

Each mode of production thus generates its specific relations of production; the basis of different forms of class society and the resulting class conflict. This has often been incorrectly interpreted as economic reductionism. But, in fact, it is the essence of a theory and method of understanding the broad canvas of historical change: otherwise known as historical materialism.

Significant as this theoretical breakthrough was, Engels argues that historical materialism was not the only great discovery of Marx.

> 'Marx also revealed the special law of motion governing the present-day capitalist mode of production, and the bourgeois society that this mode of production has created. The discovery of surplus value suddenly threw light on the problem, in trying to solve which all previous investigations, of both bourgeois economists and socialist critics, had been groping in the dark.'

Supporters and detractors alike have acknowledged the profundity of Marx's analysis of the inner workings of capitalism. However, Marx's many detractors are both unwilling to acknowledge and are simultaneously terrified of his revolutionary remedy: socialism. Theory without practice is, for Marxists, a purely abstract academic exercise, devoid of real meaning. This is summed up by the inscription on Marx's grave; namely the most famous of his critiques of the idealist philosopher, Feuerbach: 'philosophers have interpreted the world in various ways, the point, however, is to change it.' Thus it was that throughout his life Marx participated in and influenced the political struggles of his day. He was a revolutionary; an activist engaged in a struggle to change the world. Engels' summation captures the essence of Marx's activism:

> 'His real mission in life was to contribute, in one way or another, to the overthrow of capitalist society and of the state institutions which it had brought into being, to contribute to the liberation of the modern proletariat, which he was the first to make conscious of its own position and its needs, conscious of the conditions of its emancipation.'

As a result, he was deported from many European countries by governments of the day, whether liberal or absolutist. For them 'Marx was the best hated and most calumniated man of his time' (Engels).

The synthesis of theory and practice – praxis – lies at the heart of Marxism. In our time capitalism itself is questioned even by its supporters, let alone its detractors. Among the latter, a vibrant anti-capitalist movement has emerged from people who are morally repulsed by greed and exploitation. Even the Governor of the Bank of England has said that if the economic crisis worsens, 'Marx and Engels may again become relevant.' It is up to us to show just how relevant Marxism really is in understanding and changing the world. Thus we need to acquaint a wider audience with his contribution to political economy, philosophy and an understanding of class society and social change. However, these major contributions must never be seen as fossilised dogmas – as the last word on all aspects of social reality – but rather as the key to opening an ongoing understanding of the world in which we live and the way it develops.

Marx did not say it all; we, who inherit the tradition he founded, must constantly renew Marxist theory by applying it and its method to an analysis of 21st century capitalism. This is not an easy task. It requires a root and branch renewal of Marxism not just to counter its detractors, but also its alleged supporters. There are at least two obstructive tendencies which have dominated Marxist thought. One is dogmatism and the other revisionism. The former, espousing the mantra 'Marxism is omnipotent because it is true' was prevalent in the former socialist countries, failing to develop Marxism adequately after Lenin. The latter, exemplified in our time by Euro-communism, asked relevant questions but gave anti-Marxist answers which provided the ideological underpinnings for a resurgence of right-wing social democracies. Thus, the relevant questions for today have remained unanswered.

In the post-war period, communists, the putative guardians of Marxism, made the mistake of underestimating the ability of capitalism to withstand crisis and renew itself. This renewal, based on the exponential development of the means of production, has had profound worldwide implications. It has altered the relations of production in the sense that it has changed the form, although not the substance, of productive labour and thus the composition of the working class. Such changes need to be analysed and understood from a Marxist perspective within the enduring framework of the antagonistic relationship between capital and labour. Or, as Marx put it:

> 'At a certain stage of their development, the material productive forces of society enter into contradiction with the existing relations of production… From forms of development of the productive forces, these relations turn into their fetters. Then begins an epoch of social revolution.'[3]

Social revolution is neither axiomatic nor automatic. To assert otherwise would be deterministic folly. Class struggle is the motor, but only class consciousness can lead to revolutionary outcomes. It is through political and ideological struggle that the level of class consciousness can be raised. And this underlines the vital importance of developing revolutionary theory in order to lay bare the contradictions in capitalist society, and to challenge the ideology which supports it. Such challenges take a different form in dissimilar societies and varied non-contiguous historical epochs, a theme that is developed by our international contributors. Failure to understand, as well as misapplications of, Marx's method will have at least two unhappy results. It could consign Marx to the historical dustbin of 'great thinkers of the 19th century', to be studied only amidst the dreaming spires of academia. Or, if it is misapplied it could lead to a grave misunderstanding of the nature of modern capitalism and imperialism. Abundant historical precedents bear witness to this. Three examples suffice: the 'legal' Marxism of Lenin's day, the Bernstein/Kautsky revisionism of pre-WW1 Germany and the Euro-communism of the late 20th century. Thus, a precondition for renewing Marxism is an understanding of both its theory and its revolutionary essence.

Clearly there are issues about which Marx, writing during the first phase of Britain's industrial revolution, said little or nothing at all. But the relevance of Marx's analysis is not historically fettered. It lies in its application to an understanding of the political, economic and ideological realities of our era. Thus we have to consider what is new and developing. For this reason we have included articles, and in some cases transcribed speeches, of subjects of current importance: the environment and ecology, artificial intelligence, art and literature, populist nationalism, Latin America, women, social change today and the role of the modern state. All are offered with the intention of renewing rather than revising Marxism.

This intention reflects the ongoing mission of Marx Memorial Library and Workers' School. Our full title expresses our attempt to link theory and practice through the study and renewal of Marxism. Since its foundation in 1933, Marx Memorial Library and Workers' School has served the British Labour Movement and working people, in preserving its past and in providing practical education for workers dealing with current and future concerns. Our education programme seeks to apply a Marxist perspective on historical and contemporary issues. We run a wide range of seminars, lectures, panel discussions and taught courses. In the spirit of Marxist praxis, MML exists to educate and serve the only class which can lead the road to socialism. Marx is dead, but his ideas live on.

Mary Davis
On behalf of the editorial committee: Meirian Jump, Bruni de la Motte and Harsev Bains

NOTES

1   All quotes from Engels are from his speech at Marx's graveside: https://www.marxists.org/archive/marx/works/1883/death/burial.htm.
2   K. Marx, Preface to 'A Contribution to the Critique of Political Economy', *Selected Works*, Vol. I, p. 328.
3   K. Marx, ibid., p. 328.

1

Marx as a Force for Change Today

John McDonnell

Can you imagine what my press team and advisers said when I told them that I wanted to attend and possibly contribute to today's event to discuss the significance of Marx's work today? Given that it is inevitable we will have somebody from the *Mail*, the *Sun* or *Daily Express*, or maybe all three, here to record, distort and secure a lurid headline from whatever I say, the question they put to me is "What is the point?"

The point is this: first, there should be no fear in an open and democratic society of discussing publicly the ideas of a political economist and philosopher, whose works have contributed to the major political and economic debates of the 19th and 20th centuries and whose ideas are now arousing interest again. Only six weeks ago, Mark Carney, the Governor of the Bank of England, was referring to Marx and Engels: if it is good enough for the Governor of the Bank of England, it is good enough for me. To shy away from contributing to these discussions simply reinforces the regime of self-censorship that the establishment and its representatives in the media have sought to impose upon our society.

Second, I am a socialist and a member of the Labour Party. The ideas and philosophy of the Labour Party and British socialism have had their genesis in a wide range, a multitude, of streams of thought from its earliest days until now. These ideas stretch from the cultural theories of John Ruskin to William Morris, the moral arguments of R H Tawney to George Bernard Shaw, the political strategic analysis of the Fabian Webbs and Anthony Crosland to Harold Laski, and includes, of course, the syndicalism of the trade union founders of the party. Contained in this tradition, as well, are all the influences of social reform, social democracy, Fabianism, Christian socialism, Methodism and, yes, from the earliest days the ideas of Karl Marx.

So it's important to acknowledge and to understand this tradition and to explore its relevance to today and especially to the future.

Let me come to the main theme of this session: Marxism as a force for change today. I want to answer three basic questions to assess whether Marxism is relevant as a force for change.

- First, if any ideas are to be a force for change there has to be some interest in them.
- Second, they have to be relevant to peoples' lives today.
- Third, they have to inspire or motivate people to secure that change.

Is there interest in Marx's ideas?

Well, over the last decade, at the very least, large numbers of people have thought it worthwhile examining his ideas. When the financial crash occurred in 2007/8, Marx's works flew off the shelves of bookshops around the world as people sought to understand how the crash came about, its causes and, importantly, potential solutions.

Ten years after the crash and eight years into austerity in this country – the measures that are so dramatically scarring the lives of our population, and working-class people especially, causing grotesque levels of inequality and the degradation of the welfare state that was established under a Labour government – the interest in those ideas has not declined but in fact multiplied.

Furthermore, it is strange to reflect that only a couple of months ago, the *Financial Times* commissioned a couple of its experts to read Marx and Engels' *Communist Manifesto* and write a version for the 21st century. This is the *Financial Times* I am talking about. Even I found it all a bit bizarre when the article eventually appeared in the *FT*, drawing attention to the relevance of the Manifesto for today and publishing a challenging redraft for present times. It has not quite captured the sales of the original *Communist Manifesto*, but the interest is clearly there. It is also relevant that David Harvey's online video courses on Capital have gone viral. Perhaps understandably at the time of Marx's 200th anniversary, the *New Statesman* is not the only serious journal that is carrying articles like Paul Mason's on Marx this week.

In addition to these developments, the leadership campaigns and the election of Jeremy Corbyn have inspired an upsurge in political activity associated with the massive membership growth of the Labour Party to near six hundred thousand, and the creation of activist group Momentum. This has led to a surge in interest and discussion of political ideas within the party.

One example of such progress: we have been doing these economic conferences all around the country, and at one packed public meeting in Tower

Hamlets someone asked just what this PPE is that lots of politicians seem to have studied. I explained how it was the Politics, Philosophy and Economics degree. In response to this, a group of activists set up a course for people wanting to know more about economics and called it PPE, Peoples' Politics and Economics. This is an example of ordinary people drawing ideas from Marx, enabling change and education to happen.

Thus, I think there is continuing and growing interest in Marx's ideas, because in the world we face, we need to seek solutions and mobilise around them.

Are Marx's ideas relevant?

So, the second question: are these ideas relevant? There might be interest, but do people consider them relevant to the issues facing contemporary society? I think what we have seen from today's sessions is that Marx's ideas confront many of the key challenges facing our community, in particular the crisis-ridden nature of our economic system. When the financial crisis hit there was shock and widespread confusion across the City and finance sector, as well as in governments. Politicians, you may recall, told us that they had ended for good the cycle of boom and bust.

Having learnt the salutary lesson of the crash now, many fear, as Marx appreciated, that the system is crisis ridden. Counter-tendencies exist to ward off crises but can break down as we saw in 2007/8. It is fascinating how many commentators have accurately described how the massive extension of credit led to the financial crisis and then discovered Marx's writings in volume three of Capital describing exactly that.

The result was a mini industry of articles and books like Terry Eagleton's simply saying Marx was right. This has been followed by a much greater interest and debate on Marx's theories of overproduction, under-consumption and declining rate of profit, in order to have some understanding of the potential and proximity of any future crises.

Marx's original writings addressed much of what he saw in the consequences of the first Industrial Revolution and beyond. We now face what is being described as the fourth Industrial Revolution. So it is understandable that people have explored his writings to find any relevance to the challenges we face from the rapid expansion of new technology, automation and artificial intelligence.

Paul Mason in his book *Post-Capitalism: a guide to the future* draws upon Marx's description, in his 1858 piece a "Fragment on Machines", of a knowledge driven capitalism. In this heavily automated capitalist system, productivity is boosted by better knowledge and is a much more attractive source of profit than the old mechanisms of extending the working day or speeding up labour. He identifies the contradiction in this form of capitalism is that increasingly shared knowledge undermines the market mechanism. Mason,

Antonio Negri and many others now take this 'cognitive capitalism' or 'info capitalism' as it is called, to its logical conclusion.

To quote Paul, 'Today the main contradiction in capitalism is between the possibility of free, abundant socially-produced goods and a system of monopolies, banks, and governments struggling to maintain control over power and information. That is, everything pervaded by a fight between network and hierarchy.' We are now seeing time after time that network is beginning to defeat hierarchy in the development of alternative forms that pre-shadow, pre-form Post-Capitalism.

In this new 21st century our society is scarred by grotesque levels of inequality and poverty. A modern society where, within feet of the doors of Parliament, a homeless person can freeze to death. My late friend Tony Atkinson wrote a definitive work setting out an analysis of the causes of this injustice and a programme of action to address inequality. Thomas Piketty, in his detailed research for his book *Capital in the 21st Century*, exposed the obdurate nature of inequality as wealth is transferred from one generation to another.

This has opened up a new debate about ownership and class relations. Marx's definition of class relations determined by ownership of the means of production has been related to a growing debate about ownership within our society, within our economy.

The result in meeting after meeting around the country is a significant revival of interest in the whole concept of who owns our economy, who controls our economy, and what the alternatives are. It has produced a revival in interest about the role of co-operatives and the expansion of the co-operative movement, and also in public ownership under democratic control of sectors of our economy. It has resulted, in our last manifesto, in Labour committing itself to the restoration of water, rail and Royal Mail back into public ownership.

The development of an exploitative element of the gig economy has also made the relationship to the means of production and ownership extremely relevant, as gig economy workers from delivery drivers to new tech games designers explore the concept of ownership and start to develop Platform Co-ops for the future.

On the major existential threat to our society, climate change, I will not go over what will have been covered eloquently in the session chaired by Richard Clarke with Ted Benton and John O'Neill except to say that many in the environmental movement in particular have woken up to the prescient references in Marx's work to the exploitation of our earth's limited resources.

Are Marx's ideas inspiring and motivating to secure change?

So we come to the final question: are Marx's ideas inspiring and motivating enough to secure change today?

I recall an anecdote regarding the Labour Party's current policies. I bumped into a journalist last week; I will not tell you from which paper as it would embarrass both him and his paper, but he told me this. His paper had been organising qualitative polling of our policies on issues like public ownership and public investment. Focus groups were told about the individual policies and asked what they thought of them and if they supported them. Things like bringing water, rail and Royal Mail back into public ownership elicited excitement and massive support.

But here was the problem, bizarre as it was. These were Tory voters and were keen to support the policies mentioned, amazingly thinking they were Conservative policies. This takes class loyalty to a level I have not experienced for a long time.

Some time ago, others undertook similar exercises on a range of Labour policies which were proved to be incredibly popular until people were told they were Labour Party polices. It was not the policies causing issues but the Labour brand at that time. That was some time back and since Jeremy has had his impact, this is no longer the case. So why do I recount this tale?

Well poor old Karl Marx has the same branding problem. As we know his name has been used to justify some of the most brutal totalitarian regimes of the last century: regimes whose policies and actions have borne no relationship to the liberating, democratic and progressive ideas developed by Marx. The allegation is that, because these regimes have claimed themselves to be Marxist, that his analysis of society and body of ideas somehow contain the roots of this oppression. From what you will have heard today and from what you will have read, nothing could be further from the truth.

Marxism is about the freedom of spirit, the development of life chances, the enhancement of democracy, ensuring that people have the greatest opportunities possible, and alongside that, the greatest opportunity to have a say in the lives that they lead.

However, we have to recognise that to allow a valid discussion of Marx's ideas so that they can become part of debate to stimulate and inspire change in our society, we are forced to cut through this massive weight of historical abuse of his work.

I think that is what today was all about: celebrating the 200th anniversary by ensuring people understand exactly what Marx's ideas were, and the debate that his work has encouraged.

And it comes at possibly the most opportune time for a generation: after thirty years of the dominance of neoliberal theory, the ideas of 'trickle down' economics that those who hold positions of power and influence pretend will somehow benefit all society. This has been followed by the pretence that austerity politics over the past eight years will somehow enable society to be revived, and that society will be able to provide people the public services and the life chances they need, all of which has proved to be fallacious. People are proving that every day, whether at work or in their communities, that change is demanded. People want an alternative and a movement is now gathering pace which will now open the discussion of ideas that will provide that alternative.

That movement is the Labour Party, with its 550,000 and growing number of members. There is also a revived and growing trade union movement, as well as progressive movements for individual causes right the way across society, whether they be environmental, the women's movement, LGBT, all these progressive movements are now coming together demanding change.

So this is the opportunity that we have waited for – we have waited for such a long time. It means that at last we can have an honest debate about Marx's ideas, about his analysis of the world, to see what is now relevant, and to see what now needs to be developed further in this new situation that we face in the fourth Industrial Revolution.

We have campaigned for years now under the slogan 'another world is possible'. With the election of Jeremy Corbyn as leader of the Labour Party, with a new challenge to the dominant ideas of the last 30 years of neoliberalism, with the struggles that people are now participating in on a scale that we have not seen for maybe a generation, another world is not just possible, another world is in sight.

2

Marx and Value: The Enigma Code for Contemporary Capitalism

Ben Fine

The purpose of this piece, in the context of celebrating the 200th anniversary of Marx's birth, is to consider the continuing relevance of Marx's political economy, mindful that last year marked the 150th anniversary of the publication of Marx's great and enduring work of political economy, Volume I of *Capital*.

On a personal note, it is just about 50 years since I initially started reading *Capital*, which I first encountered after spending my second decade doing little other than engaging in mathematics and physics. Most of it I could not understand and dismissed but what I could understand was mindblowing. And, in the interim, returning to *Capital* again and again reveals the depth and breadth of analytical riches contained within, and especially those aspects, which had previously seemed incomprehensible and obscure if not irrelevant, became rich sources of complex insights. Marx is truly the Shakespeare of political economy!

I begin though, by observing that there are a number of relatively simple propositions that underpin Marx's political economy. First is that capitalism is best specified as a class, not a market, society based on exploitation of wage labour. Second is that it is a system that is driven by accumulation and, as such, is capable of expanding productive capacities in previously unimagined ways. Third is that it brings increasing concentration of economic and, hence, political and ideological power on a global scale. Fourth is that it is a system of accumulation that drives change in contradictory ways, given that its producers are not its primary beneficiaries, with the result that crises and conflicts are endemic. Last, these contradictions can only be resolved by the inevitable struggles within the system by, and on behalf of, working people becoming engaged in transforming that system to one of social ownership.

Now, significantly, these propositions may well be derived and motivated by Marx's labour theory of value but they do not depend upon it as such. Many other schools of more or less progressive and left thinking have offered similar propositions. So what is the added value of value theory and why does it have contemporary relevance? And what is the source of my enigmatic title – that value theory is the enigma code for contemporary capitalism?

Let me begin an answer by observing that as it develops, capitalism becomes increasingly complex in almost every area of life, in its technologies, its media, its products, its ideologies, and so on. This added complexity, whether in the economy or otherwise, has inspired the notion, even amongst his sympathisers and supporters let alone his detractors, that Marx's value theory is wrong, some way or another because life is more complex than the labour time required to produce things. With apologies for such a long quote, Marx anticipated this criticism famously, shortly after his 50th birthday in a letter to Kugelmann defending value theory as almost self-evident, on July 11th, 1868:

'Every child knows a nation which ceased to work, I will not say for a year, but even for a few weeks, would perish. Every child knows, too, that the masses of products corresponding to the different needs required different and quantitatively determined masses of the total labour of society. That this necessity of the distribution of social labour in definite proportions cannot possibly be done away with by a particular form of social production but can only change the mode of its appearance, is self-evident. No natural laws can be done away with. What can change in historically different circumstances is only the form in which these laws assert themselves. And the form in which this proportional distribution of labour asserts itself, in the state of society where the interconnection of social labour is manifested in the private exchange of the individual products of labour, is precisely the exchange value of these products.

'Science consists precisely in demonstrating how the law of value asserts itself. So that if one wanted at the very beginning to 'explain' all the phenomenon which seemingly contradict that law, one would have to present science before science.'[1]

I suspect Marx is demanding quite a lot from our children here. But the point he is making is that we cannot prove the law of value but must investigate how the labour exercised in production finds its way into society in exactly the ways that appear to suggest that something else other than labour is involved – and, indeed, much more is involved. But this has to be ordered in relation to value as starting point. That is the source of value's complexity as well as its childlike simplicity; it all occurs in paradoxical, enigmatic ways since other factors both reveal and conceal the ways in which value asserts itself.

Of course, the starting point for uncovering this enigma is Marx's theory of commodity fetishism. Let me quote again from Marx in defining commodity fetishism in Volume I of *Capital*, with emphasis added in bold:

> 'the relations connecting the labour of one individual with that of the rest appear, not as direct social relations between individuals at work, but **as what they really are**, material relations between persons and social relations between things.'

When we buy something, we do not see any of the relationships that underpin what we have accessed through simple exchange, and much the same is true when we sell something, including our own labour power. For Marx, in *Capital*, at least in the first instance, this is a matter of the concealed connection between the commodity as a product, or use value, from the commodity as a product of labour under exploitative relations. Does the consumer who turns on the tap to gain a stream of water know anything of the work, and the relations in which it is embedded, that has gone into supplying that water. Neither the consumer nor the worker can know, in the UK for instance, that as the water flows in one direction, 30% of the revenue that has been collected flows in the opposite direction in dividends, bloated executive salaries, and interest payments through a pyramid of companies that end up in tax havens.

This we know as financialisation. What I want to emphasise now, though, is that commodity fetishism is not just a fetish around labour but, as already seen, is a fetish about revenues and many other things. Capitalism positively conceals the ways we are exploited and the consequences of that exploitation across all economic, political and ideological relations to the extent to which we do not penetrate beyond the ways commodities present themselves, or are presented to us, as concealment can also be deliberate through adulterated products (think Volkswagen emission scandal), advertising, labelling and so on.

My general message then is that value theory is the code for breaking this fetishism. Let me conclude with a leading contemporary example: global warming and environmental degradation more generally. The commodity does not reveal the extent to which it depends upon the environmental conditions under which it is produced, just as it does not reveal child or low paid labour, land dispossession or monopoly and corruption. To bring about change we need to decode and reveal such relations through value theory, and organise and struggle to transform them and the conditions to which they are attached.

NOTES

1   www.marxists.org/archive/marx/works/1868/letters/68_07_11-abs.
    htm.

3

Public before Profit:

How Neo-Liberalism and Capitalist Economics are Starving Our Public Services and Silencing Workers

Denise Christie

Neo-liberalism sees competition as the crucial characteristic of social relations. Those ideas include austerity; deregulation; reductions in government spending in order to increase the role of the private sector in the economy and society; the minimisation of tax and regulation; the privatisation of public services; and the portrayal of organising labour and collective bargaining by trade unions as barriers to progress. The ultimate aim of these policies is the starving of our public services and the silencing of our workers in order to feed into this narrative and legitimise neo-liberalism.

Efforts to create a more equal society under neo-liberalism are treated as both counterproductive and morally destructive. Instead, the belief that the market ensures that everyone gets what they deserve is promoted, but try telling that to the families and loved ones of those that perished at the Grenfell Tower disaster. This will be addressed later when discussing the impact of deregulation.

The rich persuade themselves that they acquired their wealth through merit, ignoring their advantages such as education, inheritance and class – that may have helped to secure it. The underprivileged begin to blame themselves for their failures, even when they can mostly do little to change their circumstances.

After Margaret Thatcher and Ronald Reagan took power, the rest of the suit soon followed: tax cuts for the rich, attacks on trade unions, deregulation, privatisation, outsourcing and encouraging competition in public services. Through the IMF, the World Bank and the World Trade Organisation, neo-liberal policies were imposed – often without democratic consent.

The freedom that neo-liberalism offers, which sounds so appealing when expressed in general terms, turns out to basically mean freedom for the privileged few and not for the many. Freedom from trade unions and collective bargaining means the freedom to suppress workers' wages with a race to the bottom. Freedom from regulation means the freedom to endanger workers and the public in order to maximise profits. Freedom from tax means freedom from the distribution of wealth that lifts people out of poverty and invests in our public services.

I am not an academic, I am a firefighter and trade unionist; I want to share some of my experiences of working in the public sector and the impact deregulation and cuts have had on public services but more specifically the fire and rescue service.

The privatisation of public services such as energy, water, trains, health, education, roads and prisons has enabled corporations to set up barriers in front of essential assets and charge rent, either to citizens or to the government, for their use.

Rent is another term for unearned income. When you pay an inflated price for a train ticket, only part of the fare compensates the operators for the money they spend on fuel, wages, rolling stock and other outlays. The rest reflects the fact that they have you over a barrel.

Those who own and run the UK's privatised or semi-privatised services make massive fortunes by investing little and charging plentiful. Just look at Richard Branson and the fortune he has made on railways, now branching into healthcare. He does not invest in safety, good quality care or workers' wages, if he did it would suppress his profit and not fit in with his capitalist ideology.

Right-wing regressive governments use neo-liberal philosophy as both an excuse and opportunity to cut taxes, privatise remaining public services, tear apart the social safety net, deregulate corporations and re-regulate citizens. The self-hating state now sinks its claws into every organ of the public sector.

What the history of neo-liberalism shows is that it is not enough to oppose a broken system; a coherent alternative has to be proposed. For Labour and the wider left, the central task should be to develop an economic programme which benefits the many not the few and I believe under the leadership of Jeremy Corbyn and John McDonnell, that economic programme is well underway – it is called socialism.

So let us take a closer look at our public services and specifically the fire and rescue service. This year the Fire Brigades Union celebrates its centenary and we want people outside our industry to understand the pride and connection that firefighters have for their union. It comes from our understanding of the achievements of previous generations of firefighters who built our remarkable profession and made it so highly valued by society.

As firefighters, we know our history. We understand that everything in our service had to be fought for and hard-won by the Fire Brigades Union – nobody, no employer or politician, has ever handed us anything on a plate. It has been the workers, the firefighters and the union who have fought tooth and nail for those achievements.

What we have, we battled for and are still battling to this day. And those battles are against the fragmentation of the fire and rescue service. We have seen over 11,000 firefighters' jobs slashed from the frontline and the continuous closure of fire stations and operational fire control rooms – the latter of which impacts mostly on women.

Fire control operators are the frontline and gateway to the fire and rescue service yet are still not on pay parity with operational firefighters, 93% of whom are men. So even in a male-dominated profession like the fire service, it is still women who are bearing the brunt of austerity and the cuts.

And if we are to look at the impact of deregulation, then it is important that we look at that in the context of the Grenfell Tower disaster.

Action to safeguard the public and firefighters from avoidable death and injury tends to follow disasters like Grenfell Tower. The lessons learned this time must end and reverse decades of deregulation that was driven by greed and ignorance.

The Grenfell Tower disaster raises serious questions about the role of the state and the impact that corporate lobbyists have in ensuring public safety. There are many historical fire disasters that demonstrate the necessity of learning lessons quickly in order to reassure local communities that similar tragedies will not occur. But deregulation of public services and fire codes by successive governments, no doubt due to the lobbying of big business, has weakened the state's hold over fire safety.

Governments in the UK have historically taken a reactive approach towards fire safety. For the first half of the twentieth century, regulations applied to industrial workplaces alone, and were only strengthened after major fires and campaigning from trade unions.

The 1960s saw an extension of safety regulation into other workplaces – licensed premises (1961) and shops, offices and railway premises (1963) – following fatal fires in a Liverpool department store and a Bolton nightclub.

The Fire Precautions Act (1971) was another reactive measure following a hotel fire in Saffron Walden. It empowered fire authorities to enforce safety through the inspection and certification of premises. It legitimated the fire service's growing expertise in fire prevention but, owing to strict enforcement, was criticised by business leaders and right-wing politicians in the 1980s and 1990s.

Beginning with Thatcher's Conservative government, a 30-year period of deregulating fire safety followed, justified by successive governments asserting that the abolition of 'red tape' was good for both private business and public sector efficiency; there is no doubt that big business played a major role in lobbying for such deregulation.

In 2009, a fire at Lakanal House in South London killed six people; a year later, a tower block fire in Southampton claimed the lives of two firefighters. These fires have raised urgent questions about the effectiveness of the deregulated safety regime, especially in tower blocks refurbished with cheap flammable materials and ineffectively inspected.

Firefighters will always risk their lives to save others, regardless of the conditions under which they work. Historic cases of firefighter deaths at major incidents demonstrate the way that risk-taking has been embedded into the service's working culture, which the trade unions continue to challenge.

For example, a huge explosion at a warehouse fire in Glasgow in 1960 killed nineteen firefighters. Action was triggered: the service's professional associations, in particular the FBU, embedded safety in training and reviewed the lessons again in the mid-1990s after yet more firefighter deaths.

The union did so through its membership of the Central Fire Brigades Advisory Council (CFBAC), which was formed in 1947 to provide specialist advice on fire service policy to the Home Secretary. The CFBAC provided a national forum through which professional knowledge could be shared between partners. It also coordinated national policies in training, operational procedures, and standards of emergency response until it was abolished in 2004 as part of the wider deregulation of public services.

Since then, the fire service has lacked a robust machinery for sharing professional experience and clear channels of communication with governments.

The FBU's repeated warnings of dangers have fallen on deaf ears. Governments must listen to its firefighters if it is going to address clear deficiencies in its fire safety standards, and implement the lessons learned from avoidable disasters such as Grenfell.

History shows that there is a precedent for doing so, and that the Grenfell tragedy must define a new era in fire safety, regulation, investment in housing and our communities, and bringing our services back into the public hands.

That cannot be done through the ideology of neo-liberalism and capitalist economics. We must put public before profit and empower the working-class and trade union movement if we are to truly achieve a society that works for the many and not the few.

4

Every Form of Working-Class Activity

Vijay Prashad

'It is necessary that our aims should be thus comprehensive to include every form of working-class activity'. Marx, 18th July, 1871.

For a hundred years, factories and offices drew in large numbers of workers in a dense environment of surveillance and productivity. Capital, hungry for profit, saw the advantages of creating gargantuan factories and offices. The scale of production benefitted capital – by making enormous numbers of commodities, capital could bid down the price of raw materials and saturate the market with its volume. Smaller firms went out of business. The craft of work vanished slowly, as the workers had to take their place in endless lines of production, where they expended their energy on smaller and smaller tasks that added up – outside their control – into the commodity. No worker made the entire commodity, but all the workers – combined – produced them. This made individual workers into 'an appendage of a machine', as Karl Marx wrote in *Capital* (1867). The intellectual demands on the workers fell, as artisans saw their skill taken over by the assembly line and the machine. The life of workers became indebted to the factory, and the working-class found itself dragged – as Marx wrote – 'beneath the wheels of the Juggernaut of capital'.

Increasingly, capital socialised production on a planetary scale. Plantations – factories in the fields – in Malaya, for instance, produced the raw material, in this case rubber, for industrial houses from France to the United States. And then, their product – the tyre – found its way back to Malaya, where it helped cart the rubber to the port. Production socialised, but accumulation was private, and – as a consequence of colonialism – it had a distinct geographical axis. Not only was accumulation private, but it was also heavily weighted towards the core countries of the imperialist system. Workers worked to build wealth, but the workers did not see the fruits of that wealth evenly. It was this unequal system that drove the emergence of the workers' and peasants' movements.

The advantage of capital soon became its disadvantage. Having large numbers of workers consolidated in one factory allowed them to converse with each other. They would deliberate about their problems and consider how to understand the collapse of their dignity. It is in these conversations and from these actions that the modern trade union movement developed. Factories were the centre of trade union activity, because these were the places where the workers had density. They were also traps for capital – money had been invested in these large factories, and any second of wastage would produce losses to the bosses. It meant that if the workers could strike, then they would put capital under pressure. During this period, in Great Britain for instance, many of the wage workers were not employed in the factories; they were in domestic service. But domestic servants did not have the advantage of being in one factory, where they could organise together and where their strike would put pressure on capital. If a domestic servant protested, he or she would be fired. It was harder to fire an entire workforce in a factory. That is why factories became the hub of the trade union movement, and it is why the Marxists and socialists saw the trade unions as the centre of the socialist future. The focus on factories was pragmatic, a consequence of the politics that it emanated.

What is the common demand for workers today? Workers in some parts of the world can find no employment, or work for too few hours a day; in other parts of the world, workers find the hours slip by as they toil in fields and small shops. Conditions at work are execrable. It is now five years since the 24th April Rana Plaza collapse in Bangladesh. Eleven hundred workers died in that tragedy, leaving many thousands injured. Few real reforms of the system have occurred since then. Factory 'accidents' continue. Violence of a structural and overt kind against workers continues. The factories of 21st century globalisation entrap workers – poorly built shelters for a production process geared toward long working days, third-rate machines, and workers whose own lives are submitted to the imperatives of just-in-time production. Writing about the factory regime in England during the 19th century, Karl Marx noted,

> 'But in its blind unrestrainable passion, its wear-wolf hunger for surplus labour, capital oversteps not only the moral, but even the merely physical maximum bounds of the working-day. It usurps the time for growth, development and healthy

maintenance of the body. It steals the time required for the consumption of fresh air and sunlight…. All that concerns it is simply and solely the maximum of labour-power that can be rendered fluent in a working-day. It attains this end by shortening the extent of the labourer's life, as a greedy farmer snatches increased produce from the soil by reducing it of its fertility' (*Capital*, Chapter 10).

This is the condition of work today. It is what makes the question of a common demand for workers moot – so much has to change, so where does the workers' movement even begin?

Age of globalisation

By the mid-20th century, a hundred years after the trade union movement and its gains, capital had recourse to new methods of exploitation. Scientific progress helped to set the stage. New kinds of information technology, through satellites, linked the world instantaneously. Computer databases allowed firms to create inventory records in real time, so that – using satellite uplinks – if a shop in one part of the world sold a good, it would be recorded in a database in another part of the world. Stable prices of energy – mainly oil – and new kinds of shipping – mainly container ships – allowed firms to move goods rapidly from one part of the planet to another. What this meant was that production sites no longer needed to be near the market: they could be anywhere. It also meant, given the sophisticated organisation of information through computers, that firms need not build a large factory in one place. They could break up the factory that produces one good and locate them in many different regions or countries. This is known as the disarticulation of production.

Smaller factories no longer have the kind of worker density that large ones do. If a commodity is being built across national lines, it advantages capital against nations – they cannot nationalise a factory since they would only be able to nationalise one part of the production chain. The commodity chain revokes the strategy of nationalisation. The disarticulation of production makes trade unionism difficult, because capital now says that if you strike in one factory, then they will close you down and move production elsewhere. Their investment is no longer as trapped as it used to be. In other words, the new techniques of production have disadvantaged trade unionism.

Furthermore, the culture of unionism has taken a beating before the culture of commodities. People have increasingly been converted from workers into consumers. That is, the new identity is not to be seen in relation to your workplace, but to your consumption patterns. Malls and advertisements attract people of many classes to imagine themselves as someone else. Trade unionism, in this context, seems anachronistic. It is yesterday's culture, with its slogans that are seen as reminiscent of the days without malls and advertisements. Patriotism and nationalism are eroded – they are also merely lifestyles not meaningful cultural attributes. One can claim to be a nationalist without having any commitment to the people who make up the nation. The sharp edge of nationalism rubs hard against dissent. Sedition is the name of the hour. Students, journalists, workers, peasants, women – anyone who wants to suggest problems with the national consensus is seen as alien to the nation.

Structural unemployment and the widened informal sector channels grievances out of the workplace and into the streets. Survival in these streets leads to activity that could be seen as illegal – whether in the trade in drugs, sex, weapons or even barter. The existence of these activities provides the state with the opportunity to go to war against the population. The character of the state tends more to security than to welfare, to the policing of the population rather than to its care. Ideologies that argue for a smaller state (neo-liberalism) have no problem with an expanded state apparatus for security. The calculus between desperation and revolution was clear to the elite. To prevent the journey to revolution, only two paths lay open to the elite – concessions to prevent the worst effects of neo-liberal policy (which was the character of liberalism) or harsh security measures to crush the spirit of revolt (which was the character of conservatism). But, in fact, only one path opened up as liberalism set itself aside for the temper of conservatism – namely, to send in the riot police. The gap narrows between the forces of 'free trade' and 'humanitarian intervention', between the global commodity chains that wrap around the world and regime change wars that break states to create chaos. Force is, Marx wrote in 1867, 'itself an economic power'.

The International Labour Organisation's current slogan is for 'Decent Work'. The elements of the Decent Work Agenda are four-fold: promotion of jobs, establishment of rights at work, extension of social protection, and promotion of 'social dialogue' between trade unions and employers' organizations. This liberal platform seems radical in our times, when the mere existence of trade unions is questionable. The 2003 Indian Supreme Court judgment, T. K. Rangarajan vs. Government of Tamil Nadu & Others, is exemplary in its suffocation of worker power. In 2009, after a major labour struggle in Coimbatore, Jayanta Davar, president of the Automobile Component Manufacturers Association of India, spoke for his class, 'We can't be a capitalist country that has socialist labour laws'. These had to go. They have been slowly whittled away since the 1990s. A much more ambitious and confident capitalist class has reversed gains made by workers in their long struggle for self-emancipation. It has no use for liberal pieties. This is what makes the ILO's liberalism seem radical.

The ILO sets a standard that is rarely followed. It is not the Second International; there is currently no labour international worth its salt. There are barely powerful enough national federations, let alone workplace unions. Workers might not have their associations any longer, nor is trade union organising in this environment – and yet, the protagonist for the transformation, even in the 21st century, remains the working-class. Whether employed or not, this is the class that has no capital and must forage in the dark alleyways for livelihood. It is this class that represents the majority of humankind, receives little but the leavings from the table and hopes for a great deal more. Rooted in hope for an alternative is its majestic bravery in taking on the congealed power of contemporary capitalism.

What does the Left movement do today, confronted as it is by the disarticulation of production, the culture of consumerism and the rise of the security state? There are no easy answers.

Firstly, the promise of trade unionism is to build worker power. This means that one has to fight against a culture that makes people into consumers. Cultural campaigns that enrich the reservoirs of Left history and worker contribution to the world are essential. Young people no longer learn about the Left in a robust way. There needs to be a fight to introduce the history of the Left into school curriculum and to create a new cultural appreciation for the role of workers. This cultural struggle is a very important one, with trade unions needing to reach out to culture workers – teachers, artists – to help drive this agenda.

Secondly, to build worker power does not mean to only build unions in the workplace. It means to build worker power even in places where workers live – to build working-class robustness against social divides amongst workers, on caste, gender and religious lines. Trade unions can never see any struggle for dignity by workers as somehow not about working-class power. Workers cannot be powerful unless they are united. To fight against social hierarchy, religious sectarianism and misogyny is central to Left activity.

Thirdly, working-class struggles where the working-class live are essential to the re-composition of working-class power. Slums are the homes of the workers of our time. They live in congested areas, with minimal state support. The social wealth does not trickle down to these places. As a result, the workers in these areas rely upon (a) their own ingenuity and self-organisation; (b) the markets produced by gangsters of one kind or another as well as of religious orders and NGOs; and (c) the invisible heart of the women amongst the workers, whose fight to protect the integrity of their families moves them to great efforts of social reproduction. The first practice demonstrates the possibility of socialism. The second is the most important challenge, since it is here that religious organisations and the mafia dig their own tentacles deep into working-class life. They – including NGOs – are a structural impediment to the growth of the Left. But the Left will not grow merely by challenging these entities frontally. It will have to prove by its work in the arena of social reproduction that it is indeed a better alternative to religion and charity. Left organisations will need to create platforms to assist the working-class in its fights for water and electricity, housing and street services, schools and healthcare – but at the same time work alongside the working-class as it begins to deliver these services in a relatively autonomous fashion. This is a dangerous activity; it means undermining the gangs, religious groups and NGOs – all of whom have great stakes in this kind of work.

There can be no revival of trade unions without a revival of the culture of workers. There can be no easy revival of trade union power without an acknowledgment of the disarticulation of production, and the need – therefore – to build worker power where workers live if it is not possible to organise them where they work. The point is to build worker power, not factory power. Great social and economic changes are afoot beneath our feet, which will drive frustration and anger amongst workers. It is the role of the sentinels of the workers – the unions and parties – to be prepared when these waves break out, when the objective conditions of distress lead to the subjective eruption of protest.

The managers of our current disorder are not capable of taking the bull of economic distress and political confrontation by the horns; the harness of neo-liberalism is heavy, and their commitment to warlike behaviour as a reaction to unrest is too much of a habit. The social pendulum swings toward uncertainty and anguish, into which wades the hopeful Left, whose message of popular power seeks to convert bitterness to hope. 'Dekh raftaar-e inquilab, Firaq', 'Witness the pace of Revolution, Firaq'; 'Kitni aahista aur kitna tez', 'How slow, and how swift'.

5

Women, Class and Gender
A Marxist-Feminist Perspective

Mary Davis

I n acknowledging the obvious – that women's inequality exists – the question arises as to whether Marxist analysis comprehends its importance, its basis, its meaning and its relationship to class society. This is the substance of what follows. However, to clear the terrain for a Marxist approach, it is necessary at the outset to counter some erroneous presuppositions and incorrect theories.

Women's inequality today

Some have argued that women have made great progress in the 21st century, and thus they question whether it is necessary to continue the debate on women's inequality. Compared to previous centuries when women were the property of men and had no rights at all, it is clear that women's status has improved juridically. However, apart from the right to vote and own property, equality for women as it now exists is based, by an unseen process of co-option, on the successes of a favoured few; for working-class women little has altered. Despite the fact that women now account for over half the workforce in the UK, job segregation, precarious work and the gender pay gap persist, underpinned by the myth of the 'family wage' and compounded by the lack of affordable childcare. Austerity politics, having undermined public services, has led to the feminisation of poverty. In the home, up to one in ten women experience domestic violence each year; one in four will experience this type of abuse at some point in their lifetime. An incident of domestic violence takes place in Britain every six to 20 seconds. Whilst some of these issues affect all women their impact is more severe and disproportionate for working-class women. Thus, in capitalist society, the essential contradiction between women's role in social production and their role in the private realm of domestic (re)production, remains unchanged.

Analytical deficiencies

If we recognise all these signifiers of women's inequality, the popular presumption is that feminist theory has explained it all, and that feminism is, by now, widely accepted. The problem is that although the word 'feminism' has penetrated the mainstream vernacular, its speculative foundations are very shaky. Today, in the absence of a women's movement, there is also an absence of a 'grand narrative' or a putative theoretical framework attempting to analyse women's oppression. Instead, two popularly acceptable forms of feminism have arisen. Both of them can operate comfortably within capitalism and have thus penetrated mainstream ideology. The first can be labelled 'corporate feminism'. In a 21st century version of Samuel Smiles' exposition of Victorian Values,[1] it is now argued that women can break through the 'glass ceiling' if they have enough self-confidence to try hard enough. The second variant on this theme is 'choice' feminism. It champions lifestyle options and hence consumerism – you can be a feminist if you say you are one and, for good measure, wear the t-shirt.[2] Both alternatives are founded on the presumption of individualistic self-help and as such are relevant only to the few who can function effectively within the capitalist system.

Three or four decades ago, the Women's Liberation Movement generated many conflicting theoretical formulations to explain women's inequality. The contested variants would require a separate paper.[3] However, there is one newer theory which needs some examination because its impact is still prevalent. This is the theory of intersectionality; a theory which argues that people are composed of multiple identities which include, race, ethnicity, nationality, gender, class, sexual orientation, age, disability etc. Such identities, it is claimed, intersect to create a whole which is different and far more complex than each of its component parts – so far so good. But the problem is that intersectionality relegates class to a mere aspect of identity – thus defining it as a subjective choice rather than a material reality, and hence undermining the possibility of collective struggle against the very system which fosters discrimination, division and exploitation – capitalism. Without examining the detail of intersectionality theory, suffice it to say that its de-classed confusion has morphed from the now semi-ostracised diversity politics,[4] into a variant of identity politics, which today has taken on a new guise in the form of its reductionist conclusion: self-identity.

Unsurprisingly, both intersectionality and self-identity impact not only on class analysis, but on feminist theory. Indeed, intersectionality was initially formulated in 1989 as a critique of the failure of feminism to theorise race.[5] From there, intersectionality burgeoned to absorb all discriminated groups, assigning equal status to all forms of oppression and discrimination. It invited individuals to construct their own identities from an amalgam of categories. Whereas intersectionality was predicated upon a critique of feminism, the newest form of identity politics – gender self-identity – explicitly rejects feminism. It goes further by even questioning the commonly understood categories of male and female, and hence doubting the fact of biological sex itself.

The politics of self-identity

The powerful new attack on feminism and women's rights has assumed an ideological and concrete form as a result of Conservative policies which now dominate the equality discussion. This arises from the seemingly innocuous government proposal to amend the 2004 Gender Recognition Act (GRA). The 2017 Bill amends the 2004 GRA's 'medicalised' definition of gender in favour of self-declaration. In other words, anyone not identifying with their sex assigned at birth may self-declare as a gender of their preference. Whilst this appears both egalitarian and harmless, it nonetheless has important implications for women. This includes the possible removal of the protected characteristics for women enshrined in the 2010 Equalities Act, especially the elimination of 'safe spaces' for women only. There has been robust campaigning on this issue, despite the frenetic and sometimes violent opposition of some transgender activists. In contrast, the campaign on 'safe spaces' has never sought to deny the rights of transgender people to be free from discrimination, to have access to the services that they need and their absolute right to be treated with dignity and respect.

However, this is not the core issue. The largely unaddressed, underlying question in relation to gender self-identity is an ideological one. Marx and Engels wrote in *The German Ideology* that the ruling ideas in any society are those of the ruling class.[6] Self-identity, as an ideological construct has become just this – its theory and practice have permeated deeply into civil society including in the labour movement, the repercussions of which are steadily emerging. There is now, following government advice, the widespread use of non-binary classifications in many institutions – youth clubs, schools, the Church of England and possibly the 2021 Census. The Office for National Statistics (ONS), which organises the census, is currently consulting on the inclusion of a gender identity question in the next one because, according to them

> '…gender identity is a personal internal perception of oneself, and as such, the gender category with which a person identifies may not match the sex they were assigned at birth'.[7]

This reflects official HM Government advice, which states: 'If you have to ask about gender, you should list the fields in alphabetical order: 'Female', 'Male', 'Unspecified''. It goes on to suggest we should 'avoid using pronouns. You should address the user as 'you' where possible and avoid using gendered pronouns like 'he' and 'she'... You should only ask about gender or sex if you can't deliver your service without this information. If you do need to ask, use 'sex' when you need biological data (for example, if you're providing a medical service). In all other cases, use 'gender''. It goes on to give examples of 'how to ask about gender; Trans, non-binary, gender variant and gender questioning'.[8]

In other words, the categories of male and female are downgraded as is the use of singular personal pronouns. Thus, the ideological construct of gender has usurped the material reality of biological sex and has become a ruling ideology, as evidenced by the above-mentioned State support. Therefore, it has stealthily penetrated all aspects of civil society, including the labour movement.

Should this be a cause of concern? It is alarming for two reasons. Firstly, identity politics is the antithesis of class politics and thus its theory and practice should be of great anxiety for the labour movement. Secondly, the gender identity issue is of particular concern for women because it conflates biological sex and gender, and thus errantly fails to understand women's oppression. Trans people (and many other groups) experience intolerance and discrimination *but* this is not same as oppression. Discrimination itself is not a function of class society even though it is an almost inevitable by-product of the inherent inequalities within all forms of class society. Women, however, are oppressed, and the basis of such oppression is class exploitation. This is why it is impossible to understand women's oppression without understanding the varying forms of exploitation in class society – capitalism in particular. This, therefore, impels us to use and update a Marxist analysis of this hitherto almost abandoned aspect of social reality.

Women and class

Although women and black people do not constitute a class, this has often obscured the relationship of these two huge groups to the class structure. In practice, such a failure has meant that no credible alternative has been posited to that of 'identity politics'. If the oppressed and disadvantaged exist outside classes, that is, outside society, then the logic must be an increasingly atomised self-organisation based on self-identity. So what is 'class'? If we take the so-called 'broad' definition of the working-class, that is to say all who sell their labour power for a wage then it is clear that the vast mass of women and black people, nationally and internationally, are workers. This broad definition creates its own problems for socialists, namely the existence of strata within the working-class and the consequent lack of perception of class consciousness among those whose exploitation is more masked, or who have less access to collective struggle and organisation. But lack of class consciousness should not be confused with an objective analysis of class position[9]. Women in the UK already account for 50% of the labour force; hence the relationship between class exploitation and oppression has become, in our day, a very tangible issue for class politics, provided we jettison traditional gender and race-blind preconceptions about the nature of the working-class. The super-exploitation of women as workers and their oppression as women is a fundamental prerequisite for the operation of capitalism – economically, politically and ideologically.

Exploitation and oppression

Oppression, although it may take the form of discriminating against the oppressed, occupies a unique relationship within class society. It is the most important means of maintaining the class relations which support class exploitation and, as such, oppression is a function of class society as well as being a product of it. This is because oppression, unlike discrimination, is linked materially to the process of class exploitation as well as operating at 'superstructural' level through oppressive ideologies which serve to maintain class rule by dividing the exploited. This is particularly clear in the case of capitalism. The most visible and obvious divisions are based on sex and race. Focussing on the former, women are half the human race and half the workforce in Britain and are exploited and oppressed due to their biological sex, which is reinforced by gender stereotyping. This is supported by the invented ideology of femininity and masculinity which serve the profit motive rather than peoples' lived experience. Thus, oppression operates at two levels.

Firstly, at the material level, the fact of oppression is responsible for the super-exploitation of the oppressed at the point of production. Historically an inbuilt inequality within the labour force, expressing itself through low wages and job segregation, has reproduced itself as the normal process when workers sell their labour power. Its victims are the most easily identifiable workers – black people and women. All indices of wage rates nationally and internationally show that the wages of women and black people are lower than those of white males. The continuing gender pay gap shows little sign of reducing despite the government's sham concern.[10] This persistent fact clearly operates to the material advantage of the owners of the means of production – the capitalists – for whom any increase in profit is dependent on an increase in the rate of exploitation. It is hence no accident that despite conventional morality about the sanctity of family life and the key role of women within it, the labour of women is often preferred to that of men because it 'attracts' lower wages.[11] Women are clearly super-exploited, thus the increased surplus value yielded by their labour power greatly enriches the owners of the means of production.

Secondly, we must consider the ideological underpinnings of super-exploitation. The fact of class exploitation (and super-exploitation) as the central pillar of the capitalist mode of production does not in itself explain how the relations of production are maintained and reproduced. This can only be understood by examining factors which exist outside the economic relations of production through the operation of ideologies, in particular – racism and sexism. These ideologies can be seen to have a direct material connection to the maintenance of the relations of production – the central contradiction in class society. Marx defined the 'relations of production' as the tacit means by which the majority class 'consents' to be ruled and exploited by the minority in all forms of class society, with capitalism as the prime exemplar. Here the divisive ideologies of racism and sexism play a critical role. First, because, as we have seen, they are connected to the necessity of capital to maintain profit by pushing the value of women's labour power to its lowest possible limit. Second, through many centuries, the ideologies of racism and sexism have been and still are the chief non-coercive means of preventing the unity of the working-class, historically defined as white and male, thereby enabling the perpetuation of the domination of the minority class over the majority.

But it seems that the specific ideologies supporting this – racism and sexism – have operated so insidiously and so successfully over centuries, in the concealment of contradictions, that these ideologies have passed unnamed and unnoticed until the mid-20th century. Indeed a gender-blind and colour-blind approach to class politics has, permeated even the most class-conscious sections of the labour movement. Such ideologies are not simply explained by 'false consciousness' operating as an invented infecting agent. They are themselves so rooted in the material world of production that they have become integral to it. The problem is that the subjugation of women (and black people) has been historically connected with class society for so long that it has become the accepted natural order of things. The oppressive ideologies sustaining subservience are so culturally rooted that they have passed beyond naked statements of class rule and entered into the very fabric of our lives, including in language itself. As such, the ideologies of both sexism and racism have become universalised and hence disembodied from their class origins. They have thus fulfilled the ultimate goal of ideology – namely to represent the interests of the dominant class as the interests of society as a whole. How else are we to explain the permeation of racist and sexist ideas within the working-class and even within the socialist movement? Racism and sexism as material and ideological facts are central to the maintenance of capitalist and pre-capitalist class relations. However this is not to put a narrow economistic interpretation on their power These are not simply mechanisms for keeping black and women workers in a subordinate position since, as oppressive ideologies, they cut across class boundaries and depend, as all ideologies do, on their universalism. Hence they impinge on the lives of all black people and women regardless of class and determine society's perception of race and gender. They operate historically in varying degrees and forms through both the coercive and ideological apparatuses of the state. The relationship between the economic 'base' and the forms of oppression conditioned by it, is not linear or mechanical. A full understanding of the relationship between women, exploitation and oppression is vital if we are to rescue the woman question from interest group politics.

Whilst the fact of super-exploitation is not controversial, the significance we ascribe to it requires a more rigorous understanding. Such analysis 'raises' the status of women and black people beyond that of 'discrimination', to the unenviable category of 'oppression'. Their role within capitalist relations of production as super-exploited workers is woven into the very fabric of these relations and is not a chance or transitory phenomenon. This point must be stressed – it counters the 'trilogy' theory of class, women and race[12] by asserting the primacy of class in this relationship. This does not mean that oppression is thus subsumed by class exploitation, but it does mean that the traditional call by socialists for the unity of the working-class has to be understood in a different way. Unity cannot be built by refusing to recognise differences. The argument here is that the most crucial divisions within the working-class are based on race and women's oppression and that these have to be recognised as ideological practices in themselves if they are to be overcome. It is the fact of oppression which determines the super-exploitation of women and black people as workers as well as their inequality as citizens. In this respect, the assertion that the theory of class struggle is outmoded and irrelevant, is as nonsensical as calling the woman question a 'bourgeois deviation'. To seek to divide that which is indivisible is the real deviation.

Now, more than ever before, we need an approach to the 'woman question' which recognises that women's oppression is indissolubly linked to the operation and maintenance of the capitalist system; that the fight to end women's oppression is no mere optional extra, but is an intrinsic and essential part of the struggle for social change. A regenerated women's movement is a vital core element in such a struggle. The building of a broad-based women's movement and a strengthened labour movement which rejects capitalist ideology must go hand in hand. However, without a robust renewal of Marxist-feminist theory, which challenges the dominant ideology of identity politics, such a project will remain a distant vision.

NOTES

1 Samuel Smiles, *Self-Help* (1859).
2 See Dawn Foster, *Lean Out* (Repeater, 2016) for an effective exposé.
3 The best of which is Lise Vogel, *Marxism & the Oppression of Women* (Haymarket, 2013). First published in 1983.
4 'People are increasingly looking for equal treatment that respects the many facets of their identities. Everyone's identity has multiple aspects, drawing for example on their gender, age, ethnicity, and religious affiliations among other characteristics'. *Equality & Diversity: Making it Happen* (DTI, 2002).
5 Kimberlé Crenshaw coined the term 'intersectionality' in her 1989 essay, "Demarginalizing the Intersection of Race and Sex: A Black Feminist Critique of Antidiscrimination Doctrine, Feminist Theory and Antiracist Politics", *University of Chicago Legal Forum*, 1, 1989, pp. 139-167.
6 The full quotation: 'The ideas of the ruling class are in every epoch the ruling ideas, i.e. the class which is the ruling material force of society, is at the same time its ruling intellectual force. The class which has the means of material production at its disposal, has control at the same time over the means of mental production, so that thereby, generally speaking, the ideas of those who lack the means of mental production are subject to it. The ruling ideas are nothing more than the ideal expression of the dominant material relationships, the dominant material relationships grasped as ideas'. K. Marx & F. Engels, *The German Ideology* (Lawrence & Wishart, 1965) p. 64. First published in 1845.
7 See www.ons.gov.uk/methodology/classificationsandstandards/measuringequality/genderidentity, first accessed 08/08/18.
8 See www.gov.uk/service-manual/design/gender-or-sex, first accessed 08/08/18. This says that 'all public facing transactional services must meet the standard'. The gender identity standard is to be 'used by departments and the Government Digital Service to check whether a service is good enough for public use'.
9 This is not to underestimate the difficulties involved in the 'broad' definition – most notably the managerial strata, who, whilst selling their labour power for a wage (salary), are functionally linked to the maintenance of the process of exploitation.
10 In 2017, men on average were paid £1.32 more per hour than women, which, as a proportion of men's pay, is a pay gap of 9.1% (Office for National Statistics, 01/17/2018).
11 See Karl Marx, *Capital* Vol. I (Lawrence and Wishart, 1970) for useful insights from early 19th century mill owners on why they preferred to use the labour of married women with dependent children.
12 Martha E. Gimenez, "Marxism, and Class, Gender, and Race: Rethinking the Trilogy", *Race, Gender & Class* Vol. 8, No. 2: 'Marxism: Race, Gender, & Class' (2001), pp. 23-33.

6

History and Marx's Method

History to inform working-class action

John Foster

Half a century ago the writing of history in Britain was profoundly influenced by a generation of historians who had been schooled in the Communist Party and who, from the late 1930s into 1960s, worked together within a framework of collective debate. The older generation included those who knew people who knew Marx and Engels: Maurice Dobb, Donna Torr, Palme Dutt, Andrew Rothstein, A.L. Morton and Robin Page Arnot. The younger generation included Eric Hobsbawm, Rodney Hilton, George Rude, Gordon Childe, George Thomson, James Klugman, Christopher Hill, John Saville, Victor Kiernan, Raymond Williams and Edward Thompson.

They wrote history that was accessible, that sought to show how human beings collectively could change their conditions – but never did so in circumstances of their own choosing.

The hallmark of their work was to stress the importance of analysing these circumstances, of how material conditions could both limit and empower. And in a generation that had seen fascism overrun a continent and two decades of struggle to secure progressive social transformation, they wrote for those who had to carry this movement forward, the women and men who, in the broadest sense, made up the organised working-class. Defining the material conditions for change was, therefore, one that carried with it a heavy responsibility. It was not academic. Their work, ultimately at least, was for those who could bring social transformation and this made the wider surety of collective debate, international as well as national, particularly important.

Can we learn from them today? Between their day and ours lies a long period of Marxist history writing informed by sharply different perspectives – particularly from those who sought to bring what was seen as the stringency of academic discipline to Marxist study.

Importantly, however, in the 1960s and 70s, there was a temporary period of encounter between the Communist historians and their successors – important because it highlighted what were the key differences between the two types of approach and because, it is argued here, the approach of the communist historians was in key respects far closer to that of Marx himself. It is, therefore, this encounter, or aspects of it, that will be examined here. First, however, a very brief resumé of some of these successor schools to which the communist historians responded.

The search for academic rigour

The first chronologically was the French *Annales* school, only partly Marxist in its origin, which developed from the 1950s. This took over the Marxist stress on material circumstance but with a different emphasis. Its focus was on populations rather than classes: on their growth and movement, on the definition of coherent areas of geographical interchange and, against this background, the definition of periods and mentalities – a definition that increasingly took a cultural content from Foucault's periods of dominant discourse. Modes of production were replaced by 'long' and 'short' centuries and the changing configurations of regional space.[1]

Overlapping with this was the emergence of Althusser's structuralist Marxism. This demanded the *prior* definition of Marxist categories and their relationships as the basis for any analysis. To do otherwise, claimed Althusser, was 'historicist': analysis would be subordinated to empirical description. Althusser's alternative was to categorise first – delimiting ideal or typical modes of productions in terms of their internal structure and characterised by what Althusser described as their 'dominant domains'. These domains each had their own 'relative autonomy' and were differentially dominant in capitalism (the economic sphere), feudalism (the ideological) and slave society (political). The historian's task was therefore to examine actual 'social formations' and to assess them in light of these categories. Empirical social formations had to be held distinct from the conceptual tools provided by Althusser's definition of what modes of production were. Actual social formations could be composed of complex combinations of different modes.

An equal stress on the prior definition of categories was demanded by those who analysed class relations. These included Erik Wright who worked within a basically Weberian tradition and Gerry Cohen, John Elster and John Roemer who adopted the procedures of analytical philosophy. Wright defined class essentially along Weberian lines in terms of *individual* relations of exchange within markets. Within capitalism he saw these as defined by an unequal possession of, or access to, productive assets and focused particularly on those in 'contradictory' class positions. Elster and Roemer equally tended to focus, in game theory terms, on the individual and their options within complex exploitative societies.

G. A. Cohen entitled his main work, *Marx's Theory of History: A Defence*. In it he prioritised what he described as the material base of productive forces as ultimately determining the superstructure. He defined the base in relatively comprehensive terms as including instruments of production, scientific knowledge, raw materials and labour power. These, in their cumulative expansion from generation to generation, ultimately and periodically led human beings to the necessity of transforming relations of production and the superstructure. Cohen did not, however, use or endorse materialist dialectics for analysing these processes.

It was in their responses to these new academic perspectives that the communist historians defined what they saw as Marx's own most important perceptions.

Understanding human development as a dialectical process

In 1973, Raymond Williams in his lecture on base and superstructure made a sharp, if implicit, attack on the methodology of both Althusser and the analytical Marxists.[2] The base, he argued, was not to be reduced simply to the accumulation of technology even if mediated by human knowledge. It was to be understood, as Marx outlined in the Preface, dialectically as a process in tension, a constantly transformed inter-relationship *between* the technological means of production *and* the relations of production. It therefore *included* all the institutions required to sustain a particular mode of production and to do so cumulatively in the face of heightened and constantly changing contradictions. It was not to be defined simply or unilaterally in terms of technology. For capitalism today it would encompass all the manifold contradictions thrown up by financialisation, the over-accumulation of capital and interventions by the State to moderate these tensions, and to do so in face of potential class mobilisation against capital. As such this 'base' provides, as Marx argued, the material context, the explanatory key, for understanding the daily flux of language and debate, that is, the superstructure.

This defence of Marx's own understanding of base and superstructure as a dialectical process brings us to an even more fundamental issue: that of Marx's method or his dialectics. It was Hobsbawm who highlighted the importance of Marx's notes on the Method of Political Economy in his selections from *Grundrisse* published for the first time in English in 1964.[3]

Here Marx explicitly distinguished his materialist dialectics from those of Hegel and also, more implicitly, from the assumptions of Immanuel Kant – the assumptions, in neo-Kantian form, that still ultimately justify the procedures of most academic research: the stress on the prior precise definition of analytical categories which can then be used as tools to analyse a complex reality. To do so was (philosophically) idealist. It subordinates reality to preconceived categories – almost always carrying preconceptions of a particular social order.

> 'Even', Marx wrote, 'the most abstract categories, despite their validity and precisely because of their abstraction, are nevertheless, in the specific character of their abstraction, themselves likewise the product of historical relations and possess their full validity only within those relations'.

He then goes on to explain:

> 'When we consider a given country politico-economically, we begin with its population, its distribution among classes, town, country, the coast, the different branches of production, export and import, annual production and consumption, commodity prices etc. It seems to be correct to begin with the real and the concrete, with the real precondition, thus to begin, in economics, with e.g. the population, which is the foundation and the subject of the entire social act of production. However, on closer examination this proves false. The population is an abstraction if I leave out, for example, the classes of which it is composed. These classes in turn are an empty phrase if I am not familiar with the elements on which they rest. E.g. wage labour, capital, etc. These latter in turn presuppose exchange, division of labour, prices, etc. For example, capital is nothing without wage labour, without value, money, price etc.

> 'Thus, if I were to begin with the population, this would be a chaotic conception [*Vorstellung*] of the whole, and I would then, by means of further determination, move analytically towards ever more simple concepts [*Begriff*], from the imagined concrete towards ever thinner abstractions until I had arrived at the simplest determinations. From there the journey would have to be retraced until I had finally arrived at the population again, but this time not as the chaotic conception of a whole, but as a rich totality of many determinations and relations...

> 'The concrete is concrete because it is the concentration of many determinations, hence unity of the diverse. It appears in the process of thinking, therefore, as a process of concentration, as a result, not as a point of departure, even though it is the point of departure in reality and hence also the point of departure

for observation [*Anschauung*] and conception... Hegel fell into the illusion of conceiving the real as the product of thought concentrating itself, probing its own depths, and unfolding itself out of itself, by itself, whereas the method of rising from the abstract to the concrete is only the way in which thought appropriates the concrete, reproduces it as the concrete in the mind.'

Marx used the example of the apparently simple concept of modern economics, labour as a commodity. Labour of this kind, Marx argued, could not be conceived outside wider historical processes of social system transformation, processes that continued in his day and still do, in different ways, in ours: the divorce of those who labour from any access to the means of direct subsistence and the parallel concentration of such means in the hands of a minute minority that exercised power as 'ruling class'. Otherwise 'labour' in the sense used today would not exist. Equally by understanding 'capitalist' labour in its historic development, by using abstraction to move towards the concrete as a 'rich totality of many determinations', could the inner secret of capitalist labour be revealed: an understanding of how the surplus is extracted.

In terms of method this represents a fundamentally different approach to that of academic Marxism and its neo-Kantian prioritisation of concepts over concrete analysis – something which Lenin also attacked in his *Materialism and Empirio-Criticism* of 1908.

Unfolding contradiction

It was also this that distinguished the communist historians as writers of history. They wrote with the purpose of understanding the processes of historical change: the unfolding contradictions within the material base and their interaction with superstructure, with the languages of control and revolt. As historians their focus was on the dialectical process itself, on how it actually moved – not on labelling it.

This is well illustrated in the debate on the transition from feudalism to capitalism – a debate initiated in the early 1950s in *Science and Society*, continued in the internal discussions of the Communist Party History Group in the early 1960s and further resumed in debates with Perry Anderson and others in the mid-1970s.

In its first phase the debate centred on the role of trade as the solvent that eroded feudal structures and permitted the emergence of capitalism – a perspective stemming originally from the work of Henri Pirenne, reinvigorated in the 1950s by the Annales school and also in America by Baran and Sweezy, the main combatants in the first *Science and Society* debate.[4] Dobb argued, with support from Hilton, that Sweezy unduly focused on one factor, long distance trade, isolated from an understanding of the slow yet dynamic transformation of the base of feudal society in terms of the balance of class forces: the increasing inability of the feudal ruling class to extract, by state-power sanctioned force, the full surplus from the producers, the peasantry. The long struggle of the peasantry, which Hilton himself had documented in depth for the first time for England, revealed how this changing balance of class forces transformed the technological resources controlled from within the peasantry, their resulting social differentiation in terms of land ownership and the consequent emergence of wage labour relationships – a dialectical process of transformation within the base that also transformed the clash of ideas within the superstructure.

Dobb returned to the same issue in the discussions within the History Group in 1962, highlighting the contradictions generated within the base of feudal society by the emergence of small-scale capital-labour relationships.[5] It was this transformation, a class struggle for new political rights not trade itself, that brought social system change. The final episode of the debate in the 1970s saw Hilton contesting Perry Anderson's explanation for the emergence of capitalism in the 'West' in terms of the geographically specific inheritance of Roman law and its defence of absolute property rights. This again, argued Hilton, represented a partial and fragmented approach. It was, on the contrary, the emergence of nascent capitalist property relations within the base of feudal society that transformed the significance of Roman law.[6]

Contexts of working-class action

Probably the longest response to academicised Marxism, in this case that of Althusser, came from Edward Thompson in his 1978 essay *The Poverty of Theory*. 'What Althusser overlooks', Thompson wrote, 'is the dialogue between social being and social consciousness.'[7]

For Althusser and his followers this active, dialectical linkage between base and superstructure had no relevance. It was essentially un-Marxist, empiricist and subjective. Thompson's response reflected the dismay of those communist historians who had, on the contrary, seen this understanding, in its concrete detail, as the main focus of their work. These included Thompson himself, Eric Hobsbawm, George Rude, Leslie Morton and for the earlier generation Robin Page Arnot who, along with Dona Torr, played a key role in the initial genesis of the Historians Group in 1938.

In his *Making of the English Working Class* Thompson examined, against the background of growing proletarianisation and immiseration, the transformation of language that occurred between the 1790s and 1830s in which issues of class, exploitation, capitalist property rights and the role of the state became explicit. Thompson saw this as a process that involved an interplay between the lived experience of newly proletarianised workers, their development of collective organisation and the deepening dialogue

– at a number of different levels – that gave expression to this experience. It was, as Thompson put it, a dialogue between social being and social consciousness, between base and superstructure, that was not mechanical but one in which language exposing class exploitation itself played an active role. And such an interaction, Thompson argued, could only be identified by detailed empirical research that was also embodied within a wider perspective of societal change.

A decade earlier Eric Hobsbawm had published research that focused on another key phenomenon not easily captured within structuralist analyses of class relations.[8] This focused on moments of sudden transformations in working-class mobilisation – when unorganised, often mutually antagonistic populations of working people, divided by occupation, skill, ethnicity and gender, came together to form new class organisations and to transform existing ones. He examined these moments in early 1870s, the late 1880s and the years immediately before the First World War. In each period, transformations often occurred in a matter of months, sometimes weeks and then, after a period of mass mobilisation and partial victory, relapsed – though never entirely as before. Hobsbawm identified what he saw as the major trigger in each period as changes in labour markets, a sudden tightening among the unorganised and unskilled but in places where there was also an existing level of organisation and where there were workers present who carried with them knowledge of past struggles both in terms of skills as trade-union organisers and some form of socialist ideology. Later in the 1960s Hobsbawm and George Rude published a similarly detailed study of the agrarian disorders of 1830. This also focused on rapid changes in mobilisation: on language, regional synchronisation across short periods – weeks rather than months.[9]

A generation earlier Page Arnot, in terms of his own practical involvement and analysis, but in the 1960s in terms of comprehensive documentation, examined that remarkable period in British history between 1919 and 1920 in which unprecedentedly high levels of mass mobilisation occurred that, on occasion, directly challenged capitalist state power.[10]

Collectively, these studies of specific periods of working-class mobilisation had done much to restore to the British working-class movement a knowledge of a past not easily envisioned in the socially and politically conservative 1950s and 60s, and which became part of its ideological armoury in the 1970s when similar, if short-lived, qualitative leaps occurred in social consciousness.

It was also history quite distinct in its focus from the work of the Weberian structuralists largely preoccupied with resolving the position of individuals in contradictory class positions and usually doing so in quite ahistorical contexts. It sought, using Thompson's terms, to relate social consciousness to social being: to understand and relate the clash of ideas within the superstructure to the dialectic of the means and relations of production within the base. As such it required concrete analysis, in the sense of Marx's methodology, in which the dialectic was complex and two-way, acting to intensify or moderate contradictions in the base.

Conclusion: Marx200 and history in the present

This essay has not been an attempt to retell the story of the Historians Group – which has been done very well elsewhere.[11] Its intent has been to highlight, and detail, its members' responses to the new wave of academic Marxism set within basically neo-Kantian conceptual structures. This dominated the stage for the following generation and still largely does today – mandated, in part at least, by standards of academic acceptability that themselves represent an important aspect of ideological control.

These responses focused on:

- Defending Marx's understanding of the base not as static but as an active dialectical process, the contradictory interaction *between* the means and relations of production, one which provides the context for understanding the flux of superstructural debate.
- Defending Marx's Method – one which matches this understanding and requires an overall analysis of social processes to secure, ultimately, definitions that encompass 'a rich totality of many determinations and relations'.
- Understanding the role of the working-class movement, as a *movement*, one that crystallises the stage and intensity of the contradictions of the capitalist system, which carries forward the practical knowledge of those contradictions but which works within circumstances not of its own creation.
- Understanding, finally, history as process in which classes ultimately express and act out the key contradictions in human progress, a process that cannot be grasped by simply abstracting and labelling specific elements. They have to be understood as part of this continuing process.

These responses remain relevant today – because the working-class movement needs such history. They are also unfortunately necessary because the 200th anniversary of Marx's birth has seen renewed attempts to erode the integrity of Marx's work.

These include the claim that Marx's failure to complete the envisioned four volumes of *Capital* meant that he was never able to provide the conceptual framework required for social analysis.[12] This has been supplemented by the additional assertion that this failure stemmed from Marx's own realisation that his initial conceptions were flawed.[13] There are also renewed calls, echoing Althusser, for the abandonment of 'holistic' historicist analyses of modes of production as a whole – seen in their movement – in favour of looking at societies as disarticulated complexes of 'social formations'.[14]

It is therefore important to stress that Marx's approach was concrete and historical in the sense of his Method of Political Economy. In his 1964 notes on *Grundrisse* and Marx's Method of Political Economy, Hobsbawm commented on Marx's constant excitement of discovery. In the late 1870s Marx remained determined, along with Engels, to secure the most recent anthropological research and to integrate it with his own earlier work on primitive communism. For this reason he developed a particular interest in political developments in Russia and the significance of the survival of elements of communal, possibly Asiatic modes of production. But there is no evidence, in terms of his copious correspondence, that this interest was accompanied by any questioning of the basic tenets of his method.[15] Nor is there any wavering of his commitment to the need to understand modes of production as a whole and in their development and transformation.

NOTES

1 Emmanuelle Loyer, "Transatlantic Conversations: "Americanization", Modernisation and Cultural Transfers", *Comparativ. Zeitschrift für Globalgeschichte und vergleichende*, 16 (2006), Heft 4, pp. 219-228; B. Mazon, *Aux Origines de l'Ecole des Hautes Etudes en Sciences Sociales: Le role du mecenat Amercain*, Preface by Pierre Bourdieu (Paris, 1988). Between them, the Rockefeller and Ford Foundations provided the bulk of the funds for Lucien Lefebre's Ecole des Hautes Etudes.

2 Raymond Williams, "Base and Superstructure", *New Left Review* 82 (November-December 1973).

3 Karl Marx, *Pre-Capitalist Economic Formations* (London, 1964). Introduction by Eric Hobsbawm.

4 Paul Sweezy and others, "The Transition from Feudalism to Capitalism", *Science and Society* (New York, 1967).

5 Maurice Dobb, *Marxism Today* (September 1962).

6 R. Hilton, ed., *The Transition from Feudalism to Capitalism* (London 1975).

7 E. Thompson, "The Poverty of Theory" in R. Samuel (ed), *People's History and Socialist Theory* (Routledge and Kegan Paul, 1981), pp. 375-409 – quote from second last paragraph of section iii.

8 Eric Hobsbawm, "Economic Fluctuations and Social Movements since 1800", *Economic History Review*, 5 (1), (1952), pp. 1-25.

9 E. Hobsbawm and G. Rude, *Captain Swing* (London , 1969).

10 R. Page Arnot, T*he Impact of the Russian Revolution in Britain*, (London, 1967).

11 H. Kaye, *The British Marxist Historians: an introductory analysis* (Cambridge: Polity Press, 1984).

12 David Harvey, "History versus Theory: a commentary on Marx's Method in Capital", *Historical Materialism* 20 (2), (2012).

13 Gareth Stedman Jones, in C Wickham, ed., *Marxist History Writing for the 21st Century* (London, 2007); Gareth Stedman Jones, *Karl Marx: Greatness and Illusion* (London, 2016). Eric Rahim has provided a full response in "Karl Marx – Greatness without Illusions", *Theory and Struggle* 118 (2017).

14 This is the position of Jairus Banaji. Possibly the best contemporary defence of Marx is provided by one of Rodney Hilton's pupils, Chris Wickham, in his debate with Banaji and substantively in his study of the transition from ancient slave society focusing on Europe and the Mediterranean: Jairus Banaji, *Theory as History: Essays on Modes of Production and Exploitation* (Leiden, 2010) and Chris Wickham, *Framing the Early Middle Ages: Europe and the Mediterranean, 400-800* (Oxford, 2006).

15 Christopher Araujo, "On the misappropriation of Marx's late writings on Russia", *Science and Society* Vol. 82/1 (January 2018).

7

The Battle of Ideas and the Formation of Consciousness

Toward the Realisation of Philosophy

Isabel Monal

The importance that Marx gave to the issues concerning consciousness can be found and identified in his main writings during the period of his youth, particularly starting with his impressive 'Introduction (Einleitung) to the *Critique of Hegel's Philosophy of Right* (Rechtsphilosopie)'. In this early stage of Marx's conception of historical materialism, an enormous impulse was given towards clarifying and identifying the many dimensions of the role of ideas in history. Together with Engels, the further development of Marx's research led to uncovering the tools of societal transformation – the elimination of the exploitation of man by man.

Thus there existed the need for revolution – a revolution for fundamental emancipation as delineated in the *Communist Manifesto*. This amplified the urgency of a new revolutionary socialist consciousness as the essential element in ensuring the successful struggle of the popular masses, specifically the proletariat, against their exploitation. The role of consciousness in history is thus a vital precondition for revolutionary struggle. This can only be accomplished by preparing the terrain through ideological struggle – the battle of ideas. The role of consciousness is thus a central element in Marx's understanding of the materialist conception of history. Hence we must realise not just its importance, but also the variety of its dimension.

Marx's initial analysis during the years of his youth were a product of his efforts to reach a deep and full comprehension of socialist and communist ideas and theories during the struggles of the 1840s in many European countries, especially Germany and France. As is well known, he was critical of many of the theories and ideas formed at that time in this regard. During the same period, Marx was researching and writing various studies and reflections on philosophy. In 1844 he turned his attention to political economy after reading Engels' article on the subject.

There is a very well developed concept throughout Marx's writings, which showed that early on he expounded a general philosophical cosmovision (known to many as dialectical materialism), which he would then apply to society in order to comprehend historical evolution. As a consequence, Marx's intellectual development of the theory of historical materialism was a result of a simple application of a general vision, that of dialectical materialism, to the understanding of historical change. In fact, the various aspects of Marx's theory were born together in unity, constructed as a theoretical totality in a continuous linking process and – most important perhaps – with a continuous epistemological interaction between them all. In this way, new theoretical advances on some subjects had an impact on the others and vice versa. Cosmovision (dialectical materialism) and historical materialism were thus born in a unique intellectual process founded on an analysis of social reality.

Althusser's thesis of the primacy of historical materialism over the general philosophical cosmovision (dialectical materialism) ignores the mutual influence of the different elements over the others in a permanent search for coherence. Reflections and analysis of consciousness and its role in history is a key ingredient of Marx's theory of revolution and is thus an integral part of his intellectual evolutionary process, culminating in his espousal of scientific socialism. His understanding of the role of consciousness and the richness of its dimensions are therefore linked, and it is an essential part of the new theory best expressed, as 'scientific socialism'.

The theory of revolution is the soul (if we may use the expression) of Marx and Engels' conception of society and history. Criticism of capitalist society was a central feature of their political and ideological work (here, ideological is used in its contemporary sense). Today, it is not uncommon to hear that 'Marx is back' because of current anti-capitalist criticism. But unfortunately, Marx is not yet back, although it is nonetheless true that Marx's criticism of capitalism is becoming more and more appealing. It is obvious that a critique of capitalism and imperialism is an essential reference point in today's battle of ideas and in the formation and development of consciousness. Yet it is also an unfortunate fact that there is a visible tendency (and this includes Latin America) to reduce Marx to a critic of capitalism, therefore ignoring his valuable and enormous legacy of a new and essentially correct interpretation of history and society.

The tendency to limit Marx's accomplishments only to political economy is still alive. For example, the influential Frankfurter Schule concentrated itself mostly on negation, such as negative dialectics (Adorno) or the Große Verneinung (Marcuse). The tendency to limit Marxism to this kind of theoretical and political task is also a way to avoid the need for a second negation, the one that pushes the popular masses and the exploited revolutionary classes to action and to revolutionary praxis – that of revolution and the transformation of the world. Critical consciousness is valuable and necessary but insufficient; it ultimately leads to 'political abstinence', to use the precise expression of German Marxist philosopher Hans Heinz Holz in his keen criticism of the Frankfurter Schule. But criticism alone (as negative dialectics) is also insufficient because it minimises the role of consciousness.

Understanding history and society as deeply as possible constitutes a fundamental aspect of building consciousness in order to best perform its critical function. On the other hand, epistemological and historical consciousness penetrates all other functions and dimensions of consciousness. Only on the basis of an adequate and correct interpretation of reality can the class that is destined as the historic subject of change effectively play its role in the course of history.

This analysis (praxis) is to be found in Marx's early writings. One of his key theses of the Introduction (Einleitung) to the *Critique of Hegel's Philosophy of Right*: 'Theory becomes a material force as soon as it has gripped the minds of the masses'. In that case, theoretical consciousness allows us to make apparent the force of theory, that is, the correct and valuable interpretation of the world and of particular societies. The eleventh of the Theses on Feuerbach indicates that the essential issue is to transform the world and not just to interpret it. But Marx never diminished interpretation. The consciousness that guides action, which brings and generates changes in history, cannot ignore the role and importance of knowledge; it is, on the contrary, an integral part of the forces of change. Theory, that is interpretation, should not be arrogant but it cannot be at all timid either; without it the mobilising function of consciousness cannot take place, neither can it be realised. It is a question of consciousness that leads to theory (interpretation), and theory is the driving force of consciousness. Marx's thought and legacy is also a material force for today and thus constitutes the essence of the necessary forces of the consciousness required for our time if we are to transform the world.

Therefore, all these dimensions of consciousness are necessary elements of the forces that allow and bring to existence (zu sein) the realisation of philosophy – that is, the philosophy which by its nature embraces revolutionary change towards a better society: socialism. It is not a question of establishing an external link between interpretation (theory) and praxis; the necessary link already exists as an inherent and natural being of that philosophy. When such a philosophy (theory) grips the masses (the exploited classes) and becomes a material force, the philosophy of Karl Marx and his unique conception will be realised.

8

Marx's Materialist Conception of History: New Perspectives

David McLellan

In a recent biography of Marx, Jonathan Sperber tells us that Marx is 'a figure of the past'.[1] In an even more recent biography, Gareth Stedman-Jones follows a similar line, aiming to put Marx 'back in his nineteenth century surroundings'.[2] My objective, in this short contribution, is to show that, however excellent they may be in other respects (and they are), it is a mistake to think of Marx as a child of his own time – and not of ours. The study of Marx is not of purely historical interest. Recent scholarship has shown that it is, and must be, of contemporary concern.

The most immediate evidence for this is the way in which the financial crisis of 2007/08 and its aftermath is to be understood. It seems that any account must involve global capital's turn to finance as a means of shoring up its failing profits and that any such accounts are of Marxist inspiration. But as I am no economist, I shall leave it to others to explore this area.

What I want to do here is to mention two more areas in which Marx's thought is of urgent contemporary concern. The first involves his materialist conception of history. The core question here is how to interpret the classical summary – the 'guiding thread' of his studies – in Marx's 1859 Preface to his *Critique of Political Economy*.[3] Is his account of the progress of humanity through various stages on the road to communism merely descriptive (telling us how things were) or also normative (saying that this – and future – development is a good thing)? The apparent praise of capitalism as a globalising economic force might seem to suggest the latter.

However, recent scholarship concerning Marx's views on pre-capitalist societies casts doubt on this.[4]

I believe that Marx substantially changed his views here – from those expressed in the late 1840s and early 1850s to those expressed from the late 1850s onwards. In the *Communist Manifesto* (1848), for example, Marx wrote that:

> 'the bourgeoisie, by the rapid improvement of all instruments of production, by the immensely facilitated means of communication, draws all, even the most barbarian, nations into civilization. The cheap prices of its commodities are the heavy artillery with which it batters down all Chinese walls...'[5]

Thus Marx seems to think that Britain's First Opium War against China of 1839-42 was, in some sense, progressive. The same approach is found in Marx's articles for the *New York Daily Tribune* in the early 1850s. Here the view was that colonialism was, on the whole, a progressive force. And, in the *Grundrisse*, Marx backs up this view more theoretically with the statement that socialism will really be on the agenda when the world market has been established and capitalism has reached some ultimate limit to its expansion.[6]

These geo-political events led Marx to an eventual modification in his theory of historical progress. In his Preface to the *Critique of Political Economy* he mentions, in addition to the ancient, feudal, and bourgeois modes of production, one that he terms 'Asiatic'. Here, it may be argued, Marx outlines a more multilinear view of world economic development than the linear view of, say, *The German Ideology*. As Lichtheim has noted, by the time Marx came to publish *Capital*:

> 'the 'Asiatic mode' comes in for favourable comment, at any rate as far as the village community is concerned: it is valued as a bulwark against social disintegration'.[7]

Marx's revision of his previous opinion is further illustrated by the changes he made to subsequent editions of *Capital*, particularly the French edition of 1872-1875.[8] A good example would be where Marx modifies the original German which reads:

> 'the country which is more developed industrially only shows, to the less developed, the image of its own future'.[9]

The French version has an additional clause which substantially modifies the meaning. The sentence now reads:

> 'The country which is more developed industrially only shows to those who follow it up the industrial ladder the image of its own future'.[10]

This change of emphasis clearly comes to the fore in Marx's better known writings on Russia. Apart from the Preface to the Russian translation of the *Communist Manifesto*, these were unpublished in his lifetime. Concerning the Russian communes in his 1877 letter to Mikhailovsky, Marx takes issue with him on the grounds that:

> 'he feels he absolutely must metamorphose my sketch of the genesis of capitalism in Western Europe into a historico-philo-sophic theory of the general path every people is fated to tread, whatever the historical circumstances in which it finds itself.'[11]

And in his 1881 letter to Vera Sassoulitch, Marx wrote similarly that:

> 'the analysis given in *Capital* assigns no reason for or against the vitality of the vital community… This community is the mainspring of Russia's social regeneration, but in order that it might function as such one would first have to eliminate the deleterious influences which assail it from every quarter and then to ensure the conditions normal for spontaneous develop-ment.'[12]

This interpretation can be challenged on the grounds that the main thrust of Marx's historical materialism is that the emergence of bourgeois society and its capitalist economic underpinning is indeed a necessary precondition for the establishment of socialism / communism. In this view, only capitalist expansion can provide the abundance essential for a communist society. In the *Critique of the Gotha Programme* Marx wrote:

> 'the different states of different civilised countries, in spite of their various differences in form, all have something in com-mon, namely that they are based on modern bourgeois society, just that it is more or less capitalistically developed'.[13]

In other words, economic growth is essential and this can only be provided, at present, by capitalism. As Matthew Johnson said in his critical review of Anderson's book: 'Marx remains committed to the view that the productive capacities of industrial capitalism provide the greatest potential for the sat-isfaction of human needs and the development of human capabilities. His problem with bourgeois society is that it fails, hideously, to realise that po-tential as a result of its obsession with the accumulation of capital'.[14] From this perspective, Marx is talking about the achievement of a society which is based on the material affluence of bourgeois society but free of the barbarity employed in its initial realisation. In a famous passage in the same critique, Marx tells us that 'the higher phase of communist society' can only come about 'after the productive forces have… increased with the all-round development of the individual, and all the springs of co-operative wealth flow more abundantly'.[15] But there is, nevertheless, another side to the story. In the same text, Marx noted, equally famously, that the slogan that communist society inscribes on its banners is 'from each according to his ability, to each according to his needs'.[16] And clearly a society based on needs is a very different society from one based on wants. Needs are limited, wants are not. If I need something, it is always for something else. I need a watch to tell the time. If I want a gold watch, I want it because it is gold. And clearly there is a limit to what people need.

This leads me on to my second point – how Marx can contribute to our thinking about the current, and growing, ecological crisis. That this crisis is the result, in large part, of industrialisation in general and of the capitalist mode of production in particular, is clear to all but the most obstinate climate-change deniers. Capitalism has an inbuilt drive to economic growth. As Marx and Engels explained in the *Communist Manifesto*, capitalism not only produces ever-new objects in wave after wave of technical innovation: it also produces new wants and desires in seemingly infinitive measure. The resulting imperative is: expand or die. But the world's resources are limited and more likely to be able to sustain a society based on needs rather than wants.

Thus, the current ecological crisis may persuade us to re-evaluate the historical position of pre-capitalist social and economic formations. What of its political form? A co-operative socialism would obviously be the best, but some form of fascism could probably cope. The one political arrangement that will not cope is the one dominant at the moment in the West – interest group based liberal democracy in which typical solutions to environmental problems are proposed via market mechanisms such as carbon trading. Such approaches are hopelessly ineffective as they lack the social cohesion and long-term planning which alone can confront the crisis. To quote Fredric Jameson:

> 'What needs to be affirmed here is the dependence of ecological political aims on the existence of socialist governments: it is a logical argument and has nothing to do with the abuse of nature and ecology by communist governments in the East who were ruthless and desperate in their pursuits of rapid modernization. Rather, it can be determined a priori that ecological modifications are so expensive, require such massive technology, and also such thorough going enforcement and policing, that they could only be achieved by a strong and determined government (and probably a world-wide government at that).'[17]

To return to my starting point, I believe I have shown that Marx, at least in his later writings, argues that pre-capitalist social and economic formations contained valuable elements that capitalism was increasingly destroying. It is clear that, for Marx, the solution to current crises does not consist solely in the redistribution of wealth. It lies rather in forming a society in which people can live fulfilled and non-alienated lives. And it is here that both the romantic element in Marx's thought and his reflections on the values inherent in pre-capitalist social formations plays a role. Marx's whole view of human nature indicated that, even before politics and economics, our focus should be on the social possibilities of a new society. This may well include an increase in the use of technology, but as a servant to social progress and not its master.

NOTES

1   J.A. Sperber, *Karl Marx: A Nineteenth Century Life* (New York, 2013), p. xix.
2   G. Stedman-Jones, *Karl Marx: Greatness and Illusion* (Harvard, 2016), p. 5.
3   See K. Marx, *Selected Writings*, 2nd edition, ed. D. McLellan (Oxford, 2000), pp. 425 f. (Hereafter this book will be referred to as *KMSW*).
4   See, in particular, K. Anderson, *Marx at the Margins* (Chicago, 2010), and the same author's chapter in M. Musto, *Marx for Today* (London, 2012).
5   *KMSW*, p. 249.
6   See, for example, *KMSW*, pp. 397 ff.
7   G. Lichtheim, *Marx and the 'Asiatic Mode of Production'* (St Antony's Papers XIV, 1963), p. 98.
8   On this subject, see further: K. Anderson, "On the MEGA and the French edition of *Capital*, vol. I: An Appreciation and a Critique", *Beiträge zur Marx-Engels Forschung* (Berlin, 1997).
9   *KMSW*, p. 453.
10 K. Marx, *Oeuvres* Vol. I, ed. M. Rubel (Paris, 1965), p. 549. There is further information about Marx's later additions to *Capital* in vol. 2 of the new MEGA.
11 *KMSW*, p. 618.
12 *KMSW*, p. 624.
13 *KMSW*, p. 611.
14 M. Johnson, review of K. Anderson, "Marx at the Margins", *Studies in Marxism*, vol. 13 (2012): p. 205.
15 *KMSW*, p. 615.
16 *KMSW*, p. 615.
17 F. Jameson, *Valences of the Dialectic* (London, 2010), p. 381.

9

Marxism and the Peculiarities of Indo-American Socialism

Francisco Dominguez

On the 200th anniversary of Marx's birth, socialists around the world continue to benefit from his prescient analysis of the inner laws of motion of capitalism, but they also find solid intellectual inspiration in his method of politics that can be applied to the concrete realities of contemporary society in the world as a whole.

The validity of Marxism, especially his *Thesis Eleven on Feuerbach* ('The philosophers have only interpreted the world in various ways; the point, however, is to change *it*'[1]) obtained substantial vindication with the advent of the Russian Revolution in 1917.

The contributions to theory, programme and method of politics made by Russian socialists and the Bolsheviks took Marxism to higher levels. In particular their analysis of the concrete contradictions of capitalism especially in peripheral societies.

Put in a different way, Marx's framework and method is fruitful because its point of departure is the world economy as an overriding independent reality, created by the international division of labour and the world market that generates contradictions that work themselves through in unique combinations in every individual society. In short, the Marxist or Leninist truth is always concrete.

In the centenary of the Russian Revolution and the bicentenary of Marx's birth this article seeks to examine how the misunderstanding of the specificities of key aspects of Latin America's socio-economic formation led to important confusion, programmatic mistakes and political errors in the design of policies by the Communist International when applied to the continent's reality.

Impact of the Russian Revolution in Latin America

Before 1917, Latin American had developed socialist revolutionary currents and parties that were active not only politically but also intellectually. Some of these political parties, independent of events in Russia and Europe, had developed sophisticated analyses and political action for their societies. It may surprise but with regard to the tasks posed by the specific insertion of Latin America in the world economy, these pre-1917 socialist parties had essentially come to the same conclusions as the Bolsheviks for Russia, namely, the socialist revolution was not only necessary but possible, the nature of revolution even in societies that had not fully developed capitalism would be socialist, and the national bourgeoisie was incapable and unwilling to carry out the national democratic tasks.

Thus, the successful implementation of the socialist revolution in Russia confirmed the programmatic views that pre-1917 Latin American socialist parties had been publicising, campaigning and organising for. The most advanced and most elaborated Marxist analysis of Latin American reality had been developed by Jose Carlos Mariátegui, a leading member of Peru's Socialist Party, an organisation he set up on his return from a study period in Italy in 1928. He stressed repeatedly in his writings that a socialist revolution in Latin America should emerge from local conditions and practices, not as a result of the mechanical application of European formulas.

The impact of the specific brand of Marxism emanating from the Bolshevik Revolution exerted a powerful attraction among pre-1917 socialist revolutionary parties in Latin America, with many of its leaders taking the physically and politically hazardous journey to Moscow. One can gauge how positively they were impressed by what they saw in Russia by the fact that between 1918 and 1931, communist parties were established in Argentina, Mexico, Uruguay, Brazil, Chile, Cuba, Guatemala, Ecuador, Peru, Paraguay, Colombia, Panama. El Salvador, Venezuela and Costa Rica. This included Mariátegui's Socialist Party, which would become the Communist Party of Peru. This is amazing considering that the 21 conditions of Communist International membership were highly demanding:

> 'Persistent and systematic propaganda and agitation must be conducted in the armed forces, and communist cells formed in every military unit', failure to implement it was 'tantamount to a betrayal of their revolutionary duty and incompatible with membership in the Third International.'[2]

The complexities of the national and indigenous question

One of the first comprehensive Comintern resolutions on Latin America (*On the Revolution in South America*) correctly concentrates on the aggressive expansion of the United States in Latin America and the Caribbean through the politics of the Monroe Doctrine. The resolution points out that only a revolutionary movement of the working-class and peasantry can liberate those countries from the U.S. yoke, a precondition for which is the establishment of communist parties. The resolution recognises that the agrarian question is the key since the region's industrial development was minute and, therefore, the proletariat was also a social minority. Furthermore, the resolution shows that the peasantry has enormous revolutionary potential as demonstrated by the ten-year peasant uprising (1910-1920) led by Francisco Villa and Emiliano Zapata in Mexico, where the lack of proletarian leadership allowed the victory of the peasantry to be emasculated by the rising bourgeoisie. The resolution formulates an interesting dialectical connectedness between the agrarian revolution that liquidates the power of the landowners and the socialist revolution. However, a proletarian leadership is necessary in order to secure the full liberation of the peasantry by crushing the power of capital. At the same time the agrarian uprising is the only mass national force that can protect the proletarian revolution from being crushed by the counterrevolution.

This framework fitted coherently with Jose Carlos Mariátegui's conception of the socialist revolution. For Mariátegui and the pre-1917 socialists in Latin America, the national bourgeoisie, being a weak, small and dependent class below the dominant power of the landed oligarchy and imperialism, was not only unable but also unwilling to carry out the national democratic tasks to modernise society to fully develop capitalism. Thus, in common with the Bolsheviks, Mariátegui argued that the only way to carry through the national democratic tasks was by a socialist revolution led by the proletariat. However, since the working-class was so small, an alliance with the peasantry for land reform was the *sine qua non* condition for its success. A peculiarity of Peru was that a substantial proportion of the peasantry was indigenous (Inca, Aymara and other original indigenous nations) but to an important degree had maintained communal landownership through the traditional Inca grassroots village mechanism, the ayllu.

Mariátegui convincingly argued that the strong communalist, even socialist, sprit in the ayllu which had persisted for centuries, was the kind of consciousness necessary to bring about the socialist revolution. Mariátegui stated that in the ayllus 'exist very favourable conditions where primitive agrarian communism, surviving in concrete structures and in a deep collectivist spirit, could be transformed, under the hegemonic leadership of the proletariat, into one of the most solid bases of the collectivist society that Marxist communism envisioned'.[3] The question of proletarian leadership was not left as abstraction but it was given precise content: the working-class will provide proletarian leadership through a Marxist party, a communist party.

This was a novel, interesting and imaginative analysis of the strategy for socialist revolution in a backward country rooted in the concrete analysis of the concrete, historically specific situation that Peru faced at that time. Mariátegui defined the intertwined issues of the national democratic tasks and the classes to carry them through respectively as the 'national' and the 'popular'.[4] It is evident that the 'national' and the 'popular' varies from country to country in Latin America, in some cases quite substantially (especially with regard to the political significance of the peasantry and indigenous nations within given societies). Nevertheless, Mariátegui's Marxist method of politics remain entirely valid.

Latin America's 'indigenous question' in the Comintern

With hindsight, by looking at current developments in Bolivia for example, we can see the strength of Mariátegui's Marxism. By 2005 the traditional working-class in Bolivia had disappeared, especially after the closure of the tin mines and the neo-liberal policies brutally applied against workers, but also peasants, indigenous nations and the poor in general. The then socialist movement leader, Evo Morales, led a wave of mass resistance to neo-liberalism centred on the right of displaced peasants, indigenous communities and ex-miners to cultivate coca leaf. The United States forced Bolivian neo-liberal administrations to militarize the eradication of its cultivation (and deployed its own military to assist) on the back of a wholesale programme of privatisations which transformed the social movements' resistance into a revolutionary mass movement aimed at refounding the state on a socialist basis. These social movements would elect Morales as the first socialist indigenous president of this Andean nation. We can see the significance of the 'national' and the 'popular' in a country almost totally bereft of a proletariat.

Mariátegui's line was heavily contested and eventually rejected by the Communist International. In the 1920s, probably with little knowledge on the specifics, the Comintern adopted a resolution on the national question calling for the establishment of 'independent native republics', carving out a territory in the mountainous Andes for the Quechua and Aymara indigenous nations as a solution to their self-determination. The territory identified was a modern version of the Tawantintinsuyu (Quechua name for the Inka empire). The political inspiration for such a resolution was the 'Negro question' raised by the Black membership of the Communist Party of the United States and for Blacks in South Africa. The basic idea was to construct Black republics in the southern United States and South Africa. This was consistent with the Comintern's line on the national and colonial questions that defended the rights of self-determination for national minorities, including the right to secede from oppressive state structures.[5]

Mariátegui opposed this line on four bases: (a) it underestimated the strength of national identities associated with the republican states of Peru, Bolivia and the other Latin America countries, (b) the modern Tawantintinsuyu would stretch through the Andean spine along parts of the territories of Ecuador, Peru, Bolivia, Argentina and Chile that would require a level of reworking existing boundaries that would make the proposal unworkable, (c) it would have no industrial base or outlet to the sea, therefore, no economic viability, and (d) it would isolate the indigenous communities from mestizo peasants and the proletariat, and their struggles. The latter point was particularly important for Mariátegui who argued that the indigenous masses had already begun to address 'the underlying economic, social and agrarian causes of their poverty and marginalisation'. That is, they had begun to develop a new consciousness. In other words, Mariátegui had a much better and deeper understanding of the politics surrounding the indigenous question, the question of national identities, and especially, how to develop class and revolutionary consciousness in the majority peasant and indigenous population.

The final blow came at the 1929 Latin American Conference of Communist Parties at which Mariátegui presented his excellent Marxist analysis, *The Problem of Race in Latin America* (published in the same year) in which he insisted that the 'Indian Question' was in essence one of class relations, and without disregarding the cultural and political dimensions of race discrimination, stressed that its solution could only be found in addressing the inequities in the existing land tenure system.[6] The Comintern Latin American Conference emphasised the revolts of indigenous communities in Bolivia, Ecuador, Peru and Colombia to justify their line of 'independent native republics'. Mariátegui's commitment to the struggles of the indigenous masses cannot be doubted in 1927 he wrote:

> 'socialism cannot be Peruvian – nor can it even be socialism – if it does not stand first in solidarity with Indigenous demands'.[7]

To the Comintern's credit, their approach, though wrong, was not arbitrary; in fact, there had been mass indigenous revolts in the Andes led by Quechua indigenous leader, Tupak Amaru and his wife Micaela Bastidas, and the Aymara indigenous Tupak Katari and his wife Bartolina Sisa. These shook the foundations of Spanish colonial rule in Peru and Bolivia in 1780 and 1781, respectively. An idea of the strength of the revolts is given by the fact that Tupak Katari laid siege on La Paz for six months. The rebellion stretched to the Andes from 1780 to 1783.

The Comintern's line was wrong, especially the 1929 resolution adopted by its Latin American Conference, because it proved unable to dialectically integrate in a single programme aiming at a socialist revolution, the 'national', the 'popular' and the 'class' dimensions of Latin American realities.

By 1929, the Russian Revolution and the Comintern had entered into a period of internal difficulties whose manifestations in Latin America had been the 'independent native republics', the third period, and by 1935, the popular front. Their impact on the existing communist parties was negative by leading to their isolation, with most of them becoming small minority parties.[8]

The return to Mariátegui's method

The ethical dimension of Marx's life endeavour is indeed powerful. He was driven by a quest to find, in the society he lived, the inner mechanisms that would give rise to the conditions that would allow the creation of a society where social injustice, oppression and class exploitation would be eradicated. His effort to reveal the inner mechanisms of capitalism explains the scientificity of his socialism, but there is a strong moral core in his striving that became already apparent when, being barely seventeen years old, he penned an article on the choice of a profession that 'experience acclaims as happiest the man who has made the greatest number of people happy', which he ended with this:

> 'If we have chosen the position in life in which we can most of all work for mankind, no burdens can bow us down, because they are sacrifices for the benefit of all; then we shall experience no petty, limited, selfish joy, but our happiness will belong to millions, our deeds will live on quietly but perpetually at work, and over our ashes will be shed the hot tears of noble people.'[9]

Interestingly, the Latin American Liberator, Simón Bolívar, in his Angostura Address on 15th February 1819, stated that:

> 'the most perfect system of government is that which results in the greatest possible measure of happiness and the maximum of social security and political stability'.[10]

Hugo Chávez, the revolutionary leader of Bolivarian Venezuela, drew inspiration in the brand of socialism that he popularised among millions of Venezuelans from three 19th century iconic political leaders and intellectuals, namely, Simón Bolívar, Simon Rodriguez and Ezequiel Zamora. The first, the Liberator of Latin America *par excellence*, was the head of huge armies that fought and defeated the Spanish, leading to the independence of five countries (Venezuela, Colombia, Ecuador, Peru and Bolivia). He left a gigantic legacy of letters, proclamations, articles, and speeches that are still an inspiration for progressive and revolutionary ideas. Simon Rodriguez was young Bolívar's personal tutor, a radical socialist influenced by Proudhonian ideas which he instilled in his tutee. And Ezequiel Zamora was a political and military leader of the revolutionary forces in the Federal War (1859) during which he liberated and armed Black slaves and indigenous communities to defeat the oligarchy so as to eradicate the highly iniquitous latifundia system.[11] Chavez christened them as the 'tree of the three roots', the sources of Chavismo, whose inspirational and mobilizing force for socialism continues to reverberate among millions of Venezuelans and Latin Americans today. Chavez clearly understood how to draw out the collectivist thirst for justice among the millions of poor Venezuelans, the driving force of Bolivarian socialism.

To this gallery of historic heroes, Hugo Chávez added a few more that hitherto had been almost invisible. He vindicated and glorified, amongst many others, indigenous leader, Guaicaipuro, José Leonardo Chirinos, Pedro Camejo and Negra Hipolita. Guaicaipuro was an indigenous leader who in the 16th century organised fierce and successful military resistance against the Spanish conquistadors; his forces drove them from Los Teques, a region in Caracas, and kept them out for nearly a decade. He was eventually defeated, captured and died fighting in battle. José Leonardo Chirino was the leader of a combined indigenous and Black slaves' insurrection in 1795 whose aim, inspired by the Black rebellion in Haiti, was to establish a Republic, the abolition of slavery, the abolition of privileges and equality among classes. He was defeated, captured and executed by hanging. Pedro Camejo, a freed slave, was drafted by the Spanish to fight against Simón Bolívar's armies, but he eventually joined Bolívar's forces and died heroically in the famous battle of Carabobo in 1821, at which the Spanish suffered a decisive defeat. Negra Hipolita, a Black slave, was Simón Bolívar's wet nurse because Bolívar's mother's health was very precarious. In Bolivarian Venezuela, statues of these iconic figures have been erected everywhere: streets, plazas, buildings and institutions have been named after them; Venezuelan bank notes and coins carry their images; and their contribution to the country's history is compulsory in the national curriculum. As Mariátegui did, Chávez understood the 'national' and the 'popular'.

It is on the back of this rich tradition of the struggle for the nation, equality, and social justice that Chávez has didactically inspired millions of Venezuelans whose synthesis is the fight for the Bolivarian socialism of the 21st century.

As in Venezuela, one can find Mariátegui's Marxist method of politics by the synthesis of the rich tradition of struggle into a socialist programme of structural political and socio-economic transformation in many a Latin American country. Thus, for example, the politicising power of Evo Morales' speeches to the Bolivian masses (of which indigenous people represent 65% of the total population) is huge, when he tells them that as the Spanish were publicly quartering Aymara's 1780 indigenous rebellion leader Tupak Katari, he would have said 'they can kill me now, but I will come back as millions'. This is especially powerful when Morales closes the sentence with: 'We have come back as millions'.

Conclusion

Progressive Latin America is currently under a vicious and systematic attack that is being organised, led and financed by Washington, out of which it has suffered some serious setbacks and defeats. The progressive governments of Honduras and Paraguay have been forcefully overthrown in 2009 and 2012, respectively; the right-wing have come to office in Argentina in 2015; Dilma Rousseff, president of Brazil, was impeached and her government ousted in 2016 and through the use of 'lawfare', former president Lula is in prison on totally fabricated charges; Venezuela has been under a vicious all-out assault through economic warfare reminiscent of what was done to Salvador Allende in Chile in the 1970s; the FSLN government of Nicaragua is being subjected to economic warfare and a wave a horrible violence perpetrated by armed thugs of the extreme right who are financed with Washington's dollars; and a programme of violent destabilisation seems to have been started in Bolivia.

In terms of our discussion in this article, there would appear to exist a strong correlation between the ability to resist imperialist aggression and levels of structural transformation of the state among individual Latin American countries. The level of pressure and aggression, though the nasty, well-organised and vicious offensive that the Workers' Party government of Dilma Roussef was subjected to, represents a fraction of what has been inflicted on Bolivarian Venezuela. U.S. imperialism and Brazil's bourgeoisie countered not only with the media, but also with congress, the judiciary and the armed forces to carry out the 'constitutional coup' against Dilma, a context that is simply not possible in Venezuela.

Thus, the key to progress the socialist transformation of a Latin American nation is not the level of socialisation of the means of production, important as this is, but the transformation of the class nature of the state. Furthermore, the state can be transformed and a socialist revolution can be carried out provided the proletariat, as Mariátegui argued, is capable of furnishing the non-proletarian dispossessed masses, especially the peasantry and the indigenous nations, with clear political leadership.

Proletarian political leadership is not only possible but necessary since mobilising what Mariátegui identified as the 'national' and the 'popular' has the function of carrying through the national democratic tasks which the domestic bourgeoisie is incapable and unwilling to implement. These tasks can only be completed and defended by carrying out a socialist revolution.

The concrete analysis of the concrete situation is the only way to fruitfully apply the Marxist method about which Lenin was unequivocal:

> 'One of the basic principles of dialectics is that there is no such thing as abstract truth, truth is always concrete...'[12]

When it came to Latin American political developments, Marx himself, by drawing conclusions out of some abstract truth which he himself had developed, dramatically erred. Marx described Simón Bolívar as 'an imitation of Napoleon III, or more precisely, some sort of Bonapartist dictator', and the 'dastardly, most miserable and meanest of blackguards'. Although in a letter to Engels he admitted that this was an exaggeration, he corrected his view by suggesting that 'Bolívar is a veritable Soulouque', the slave-turned-emperor of Haiti who Engels and Marx used to ridicule Napoleon III.[13]

Furthermore, on the occasion of the United States invasion of 1847, Engels wrote:

> 'We have witnessed the conquest of Mexico and we have rejoiced at it...It is to the interests of its own development that Mexico will in the future be placed under the tutelage of the United States'.

Later on, Engels expanded his views of the U.S. war against Mexico in 1845-1848:

> 'Will Bakunin accuse the Americans of a "war of conquest", which, although it deals with a severe blow to his theory based on "justice and humanity", was nevertheless waged wholly and solely in the interest of civilization? Or is it perhaps unfortunate that splendid California has been taken away from the lazy Mexicans, who could not do anything with it?'[14]

Thus, the moment an abstract truth substitutes the concrete analysis of the concrete situation (in the cited cases of Engels and Marx, the abstract categories of 'Bonapartism' and 'the development of the productive forces' are the causes of the mistakes), any analysis can easily err. The Communist International's rejection of Mariátegui's Marxist method of understanding how the 'national' and the 'popular' could be mobilised and coherently integrated into a programme of socialist revolution, and instead the rather mechanical application of policies on the national question to Latin America, had clear negative consequences.

The only way to successfully apply the Marxist method is by the Lenin-Mariátegui approach, so fascinatingly unfolding in the socialist revolutions in Latin America. This much we owe to the founder of modern communism, Karl Marx, in the 200th anniversary of his birth.

NOTES

1   Karl Marx, *The German Ideology: Including Theses on Feuerbach and an Introduction to the Critique of Political Economy* (Prometheus Books, 1998).

2   Jane Degras, *The Communist International 1919-1943 Documents*, https://www.marxists.org/history/international/comintern/documents/volume1-1919-1922.pdf, accessed on 21st June 2018.

3   Mariátegui, Jose, "El problema de las razas en la America Latina", in *Ideologia y Politica*, https://www.marxists.org/espanol/mariateg/oc/ideologia_y_politica/paginas/tesis%20ideologicas.htm, accessed 21st June 2018.

4   Mariategui discussed the indigenous question in detail in his seminal *Seven Interpretive Essays of Peruvian Reality* (Biblioteca Amauta, Lima, Peru, 1928).

5   Marc Becker, "Mariátegui, the Comintern, and the Indigenous Question in Latin America" in *Science & Society*, Vol.70 (October 2006), pp. 450-479.

6   Marc Becker, op. cit., p. 451.

7   Marc Becker, op. cit., p. 453.

8   It would be thoroughly unfair to attribute the lack of success of the Latin American Communist parties solely to the 1920-1929 resolutions of the Comintern: repression, the Cold War and demonisation also played an important part.

9   Karl Marx, "Reflections of a young man on the choice of a profession" (1835), https://libcom.org/book/export/html/54186, accessed 22nd June 2018.

10 John Lynch, *Simon Bolivar and the Age of Revolution*, University of London Institute of Latin American Studies, Working Papers, p. 7.

11 See Richard Gott, *Hugo Chavez and the Bolivarian Revolution* (Verso Books, 2011), especially Part Four, pp. 119-142.

12 Lenin, V.I., *One Step Forward, Two Steps Back*, Marxists Internet Archive, https://www.marxists.org/archive/lenin/works/1904/onestep/r.htm, accessed 24th February 2018.

13 Jose M. Aricó, *Marx and Latin America*, (Brill, Leiden, Boston, 2014), p. 53.

14 Ronaldo Munck, "Marx and Latin America", *Bulletin of Latin American Research* Vol.3, No.1 (Jan 1984), pp. 141-142.

10

Artificial Intelligence and the Abstraction of Cognitive Labour

Alan F. Blackwell

Many commentators on labour are concerned about the potential impact of artificial intelligence (AI) technologies for the 21st century economy. The usual concern is the possibility that paid employment opportunities will disappear through replacement of human workers by artificially intelligent machines. However, concern for loss of jobs is a familiar narrative, in which the special characteristics of AI are not relevant. All technological advances, since prehistoric times, have resulted in changes to human work.

Human work has already changed in response to technical innovations from relatively recent such as cashless transactions, robotic assembly, bulk transport or earthmoving, to the ancient such as mechanical weaving, harvesting, ploughing and threshing, and the prehistoric – iron, stone and wooden tools.

This paper does not repeat standard concerns about mechanisation and workplace change. Instead, it addresses the question of what is special about AI, and the ways in which changes due to AI might do more than simply repeat the dynamics of earlier waves of mechanisation and automation since prehistoric times. This argument depends on two phenomena that appear to be new in the 21st century. The first is the special nature of AI, in its relation to human thought and imagination. The second is the specific characteristics of the 21st century economy that relate to information technologies.

In the following sections, each of these is discussed in turn to establish critical definitions and the key concerns that arise from them. The final part of the paper then considers the consequences that arise from the abstraction of cognitive labour in particular.

What is artificial intelligence?

Public commentary and speculation about AI conflates a rather diverse range of technical and commercial activity, in which there is no single definition that unproblematically encompasses this whole range. There are three common kinds of definition – I address each of these below, followed by a fourth that is less familiar in popular discourse, but more appropriate to Marx's bicentenary.

A first possible definition is the one proposed by pioneering computer scientist Alan Turing, now popularly described as the 'Turing Test'. Turing's purpose was, within a positivist frame, to avoid the need to define intelligence in philosophical enquiry. The nature of intelligence, of the mind or soul, is one of the oldest questions in metaphysical enquiry, but such questions are not necessarily significant to labour or to economics. Of slightly more relevance is the way that Turing's test has changed from philosophical exercise into a competition, having rewards for the winner – this is an issue that I will return to.

A second possible definition of AI, sometimes considered flippant but probably more relevant to current policy debate than the Turing Test, is that AI is the field of research that tries to make computers work the way they do in the movies. My own impression as a professor of computer science is that this is more true than funding bodies might wish. Many young AI researchers do indeed establish their research questions and personal ambitions on the basis of science fiction they have read or seen. So in this case, AI is a branch of speculative fiction, continuing many years of speculative fictions in which manmade artefacts are given minds or souls, including the legends of the Golem, Pygmalion and Frankenstein, movies from *Metropolis* to *Ex Machina*, or the quasi-religious idea that we might make a machine so powerful that it becomes a 'singularity' – a kind of god figure that would control us all.

A central theme in these fictions is retribution for hubris. The creator of these artificial beings suffers retribution for presuming to create a soul, retribution for aspiring to create a god, or in the case of *Metropolis, Ex Machina* and many others, retribution for sexual desire of an artificial woman. These stories depend on classic narratives of gender, power and punishment, all of which correspond to important questions in Marxist analysis, but are perhaps no more novel than any other uses of religious fantasy to reinforce social structures.

A third definition of AI is that it is simply an engineering technique, pertaining to a particular class of algorithms. Professional software engineering consists of applying algorithms to practical problems, and much of computer science education consists of learning a practical 'toolbox' of these algorithms and how they can be used. By convention, some algorithms are described as AI algorithms and some are not. However, the technical distinctions change over time. Many algorithms that were fundamental to AI

50 years ago (such as goal-directed search) are today considered absolutely routine, while the AI algorithms of today are likely to be considered routine in another five to ten years. The steady trend is sometimes acknowledged by AI researchers in a jokey manner through the saying that 'if it works, it isn't AI'. So this particular definition leads to the rather boring conclusion that AI is simply one among many techniques known to engineers, having no special interest or relevance for Marxist analysis.

Each of the above three definitions is well known to AI researchers, whether or not the distinctions between them are properly understood by excitable commentators. However, there is a fourth possible definition, especially relevant in the context of the Marx bicentenary, found in the words of Marx himself in his reflection on machines:

'Rather it is the machine which possesses skill and strength in place of the worker, is the virtuoso with a soul of its own in the mechanical laws acting through it'. (*Grundrisse*, p. 693).

This sentence, and the passage in which it appears, are quite remarkable for the degree to which a 19th century writer has anticipated the 21st century definitions that I have discussed above. Marx refers to the action of mechanical laws: algorithms are nothing more or less than mechanical laws by which a skilled procedure is performed. In the absence of computer science terminology, Marx could hardly have done better in summarising the key issues of AI. The philosophical and imaginative concerns of Turing and the science fiction writers are anticipated in uses of the term 'virtuoso' and 'soul' in relation to a machine, while the potential for those faculties to be achieved through 'mechanical laws' expresses the engineering character of AI algorithms.

We can admire Marx's prescience, which may well have been influenced by awareness in London of the pioneering work by Babbage and Lovelace, which extended the data-encoding principles of the Jacquard loom to automation of intellectual tasks. However the critical question for the modern reader, as I will argue, is the specific technical means by which the action of mechanical laws can stand in place of the human worker. To quote again from the *Grundrisse*:

'Once adopted into the production process of capital, the means of labour passes through different metamorphoses, whose culmination is the machine, or rather, an automatic system of machinery, set in motion by an automaton, a moving power that moves itself; this automaton consisting of numerous mechanical and intellectual organs, so that the workers themselves are cast merely as its conscious linkages'.

The references to 'casting' and 'metamorphoses' in this passage can be considered as varieties of abstraction. This is abstraction, not only in the economic sense applied in much of Marx's writing, but also abstraction in the sense used by computer scientists – where a more complex phenomenon is represented by a simpler mathematical characterisation of data or processes. If the labour of the worker can be reduced to an abstraction of activity, it can then be determined and regulated by the movement of the machinery. This is a phenomenon that seems perfectly familiar to all of us today. Marx's view of the relation between people and machines anticipated a central characteristic of 21st century living.

The commodities of abstraction

If we pursue this equation between the abstraction of labour in the 19th century industrial era, and the abstractions of computer science in the 21st century, what kinds of economic manifestation might we see? Marx recognised that monetary systems are grounded in a fetishised commodity (for example the gold standard) where that commodity is itself extracted through labour (in that case, gold mining). However, there are several alternative ways of describing the more abstract commodities of the contemporary era, and I consider each of them, with their labour implications, in turn.

1. In an information economy, information might be seen as a fetishised commodity.
2. In a knowledge economy, knowledge might be seen as a fetishised commodity.
3. In a reputation economy, reputation might be seen as a fetishised commodity.
4. In an attention economy, human attention might be seen as a fetishised commodity – and it is this alternative that seems likely to be most fruitful as I will discuss below.

To start with, let us consider the implications of treating information as a commodity. In the technical sense of the word as used by computer scientists, information is a physical quantity – it measures the number of bits of data that are being stored or transmitted. Physical quantities in themselves are indeed abstract, but they have no intrinsic value. To ask what information is worth would be no more sensible than to ask "what is length worth" or "what is mass worth"? If I say that "my book has 237 pages", I have given you information, but not necessarily value.

Nevertheless, we have seen a recent attempt to commoditise numbers themselves in the Bitcoin digital currency. A Bitcoin is literally just a number. It happens to be a big number that has never been written down before, and if you are the first to 'write it down' (through Bitcoin 'mining'), this act is considered to create value. However a Bitcoin is a sequence of digits that as far anyone can tell (and this is important) are random. Bitcoin emphasises the extent to which information in itself is not valuable, instead drawing attention to the technologies that we use to store, process and transmit information. It is significant that the owners of technology control the economy. If we look beyond the purely synthetic notion of 'value' in numerical financial instruments, it is more important to consider what information encodes or measures. This can also be a fetishised commodity – in my list of alternatives – potentially including knowledge, reputation or human attention.

Let us first consider the commodification of knowledge in the knowledge economy – for example, the knowledge contained in books such as this one. In the case of my own intellectual labour, often devoted to writing such books or other academic papers, it might appear that I am creating value. But in the engineering sense, information is actually the measure of a communication channel, meaning that the value of such knowledge is dependent on someone reading it at the other end of the channel. This is not guaranteed – like many academics, I am occasionally responsible for writing that will be read only by my own students (if at all).

Perhaps more significant are information stores like Wikipedia, which represents both a large amount of information (and readers receiving that information), and also huge amounts of labour – unpaid labour. Nobody is paid for contributing to Wikipedia, so we might reflect on the extremity of a capitalist system in which a commodity is generated by labour with no wages at all. Of course, the source of this particular paradox relates to reputation and attention, to be considered below.

However, readers may have noticed that much of the knowledge in Wikipedia also does not seem very valuable in an economic sense. Some readers might not be interested in the season scores of a baseball team in a small American town, and indeed the residents of that town may be similarly uninterested in things that interest others. So, as with information, knowledge is not an absolute. In many cases, we consider information to be valuable in relation to the reputation of the person who has generated that knowledge – and perhaps also the enhanced reputation that you may gain from emulating them. And this of course is how we construct academic disciplines, not according to a predetermined structure of the world but to the social structures of reputation and admiration.

If knowledge is, to a large extent, a byproduct of reputation, then the reputation economy appears more significant. Many of the hyper-capitalist digital systems, including Deliveroo, Uber, airBnB, eBay or YouTube, involve human relational labour that is quantified in terms of reputation points. The most dedicated editors of Wikipedia are also recognised with reputation awards, and of course most forms of social media constantly quantify the influence or reach of each of their users.

Perhaps the most advanced, most commodified, of reputation economies is the academic citation market. Working academics in the UK today literally work for, and their universities are paid in, reputation points – counted not only through government or peer review, but by online information systems that are structured through monopoly interests. There have been counter-proposals that the academic reputation economy should be replaced by one that rewards universities for the contributions they have made to society, whether through entertainment or 'impact'. But contributions judged and recorded through monopoly infrastructure providers raise serious questions about whether excess value has been extracted or whether there has been due reward for labour.

This leads to the last of my four alternative perspectives for characterising the commodity that underlies the information economics of AI – the economy of attention. It relies on the observation that the labour of the information economy is not primarily associated with operation of physical machinery or manipulation of manufactured objects, but with the extent to which abstraction of labour itself is being amassed.

In this perspective, we consider any items of data stored on a computer that have been extracted from a person interacting with that computer. This data represents the time that a person has spent interacting with a screen or a keyboard – and can be quantified as a fraction of their whole life. When users attend to computers, they are constantly delivering information through the screen controls and the keyboard. This is rather different from the market messages of the media industry, which presume that they are delivering a product to you.

It is generally understood that advertising has value in the degree to which an advertiser gains people's attention, but this is a relatively trivial way of understanding the phrase 'attention economy'. It assumes that the advertiser is delivering something to the viewer, and that to some extent that viewer is receiving a service. But this conventional media industry model pays no attention to the fact that information can also flow in the other direction. In digital media, the user is not simply viewing, but providing information by pressing keys, entering Facebook updates, sending Whatsapp messages, or clicking 'like' buttons. The cliché associated with these business models is that, if you are not paying for the product you receive, then you are the product.

When we receive something for free from these companies, what are we giving them in return? We are giving our attention as intelligent actors. We are giving seconds, minutes or, more often, hours of our lives investing intelligence into the digital ecosystem – trying to make computers do the things that we would like them to do. We are not (of course) paid for any of this time. More worryingly, there is no constraint on companies collecting the intelligent data we supply, in order to simulate some kind of artificial intelligence.

The technical details of the ways that human attention is harvested from users and resold as AI is often (intentionally) obscured, but there is one particularly dramatic illustration of the basic principle that is carried out in plain sight. This is a literal commoditisation of human intelligence through the Amazon Mechanical Turk service (often called AMT) and similar 'crowd-sourcing' platforms that have followed it.

These systems are brokerages that buy and sell 'human intelligence tasks' or HITs. AMT will pay a human 'Turker' one or two pennies for a small task – some judgement or decision requiring a small amount of intelligence – in fact, exactly the same kind of intelligence that many AI programs are expected to deliver by themselves. In many cases, what has actually happened is that the program has, across the network, made a request for a component subroutine to make a judgement task. However, this 'component' is not a piece of software, but a human who is paid for devoting a few seconds of their attention to things a computer might have done.

It almost seems like a hoax to call the result of such a system AI, given that the actual intelligence came from a human. Indeed the name 'Mechanical Turk' is a rather brazen reference to the famous 18th century hoax of that name: supposedly a chess-playing automaton, but actually a machine whose actions were really carried out by a chess expert hiding inside. In the digital age, these machines (both the 18th century chess player and the 21st century 'Turker') can be seen as anticipating the observation by Marx that the workers themselves are cast merely as its conscious linkages.

The moral hazards of artificial intelligence

Consideration of the attention economy highlights the ways that AI is often delivering information that abstracts human lives and labour. This is perhaps no more or less than any other capitalist production system, but AI also involves a good deal of obfuscation through reference either to the fictions and fantasies of artificial intelligence or to the philosophical claims of whether machines may or may not be self-aware, ethical actors. Many of our policy makers, parliamentarians, newspapers – even union activists – are distracted by those apparently exciting philosophical questions, not realising that in fact these algorithms rely more or less directly on the abstraction of human cognitive labour.

This leads to a number of important questions we ought to be asking. Digital activists are often libertarians, primarily concerned with questions of privacy and surveillance, and with the increasingly frequent scandals revealing social media companies' influence over democratic elections or government. Privacy and surveillance are indeed important because people need private space in which to individuate themselves, space in which to create their personal identity. Being private is part of being a human. But largely the anxieties underlying those questions are the paranoia of the rich. For the poor, privacy is already a luxury and it makes little difference to them who is collecting their Facebook data.

A more significant question may be, if an AI system is observing hundreds of millions of human actions and replaying those actions through statistical correlations as 'neural networks' do, then who should be acknowledged as the author? Is it the programmers who harvested the data or the workers (paid or unpaid) whose attention has been harvested? More mischievously, companies can wield the fictional claims of artificial intelligence to claim that the machine has become self-aware and is acting on its own. If that really were the case, then nobody needs to be recognised or rewarded, because the owner of the machine is the owner of its labour (in a revival of the logic of slavery, where ownership of the worker implies ownership of the results of his labour). From this perspective, when companies indulge in philosophical speculation about the 'autonomy' or 'agency' of AI systems, their contributions appear to intentionally obscure the labour of those humans who have actually been involved in the operation of the AI, and thus, in the terms of Marx, have been reduced to 'conscious linkages' in the machine that moves itself.

Underlying these moral and economic concerns is the fact that recognition of authorship is a fundamental principle in the Universal Declaration of Human Rights (Article 27). However, the Article refers specifically to scientific, literary or artistic production, which raises the question of how to interpret those terms in the attention economy of cognitive labour. In the case of Wikipedia, although the authors are conventionally anonymous, pages often include substantive scientific substance, as well as original and laborious editorial work. If the editorial work involved in maintaining Wikipedia were to be mechanised, then this might be the criterion by which a lawyer could claim that the mechanical nature of the editing did not constitute a literary work, while a human editor makes creative judgements that warrant recognition of authorship. This recapitulates the earlier definition from computer science that 'if it works, it isn't AI' – if mechanical work is not authored, then authors cannot be mechanical.

The question of whether creative human editorial work deserves to be recognised as 'literary' (in some sense), and hence deserving recognition of authorship, applies to cases that are even more commonplace than that of Wikipedia. When you start typing into a search engine, and it helpfully completes the phrase that you might be wanting to type, this is a familiar and welcome everyday kind of 'AI'. So how does this 'AI' actually work? Most of us understand that the suggestion you see was previously typed by somebody else, and that the system is simply replaying their typing for you to use. What if that person had a particularly insightful way of framing their problem, if it had taken ten or twenty minutes to think of just the right way to phrase it? Some of these suggestions are elegant aphorisms, of the kind that would certainly have been attributed to an author – but no attribution is offered by the search engine. In fact, when I type the words 'It is a ...' into my own web browser, the search engine immediately suggests the phrase '... truth universally acknowledged'. There is no attribution of authorship, despite the fact that this phrase is clearly the work of a specific author. What if the author is someone less well known? Search engines routinely record all the keystrokes made by their users, store them in databases and give them to other people, with no payment or recognition.

Most search engine users have some awareness of the deal they are making (and indeed, have been persuaded that these deals, hidden in hundreds of pages of 'terms of service' and 'end-user licence agreements', represent more-or-less voluntary assent to an unavoidable situation). Nevertheless, enforced assent does not excuse those companies from the potentially unethical and inequitable implications of the way their systems operate.

Although search engine users have no option but to accept the terms of service offered, why do people devote so much labour and attention to joint projects such as Wikipedia? To a large extent, these projects build on the philosophy and rhetoric of 'open source', in which collective voluntary action can create a new public good. Originally developed by the idealists of the Free Software Foundation and similar organisations emerging from academic computer science departments, legal principles of joint ownership have been formalised (and applied to Wikipedia) through the principles of Creative Commons.

To historians of capital and labour, the use of the term 'Commons' immediately raises the question of whether these 21st century commons might be subject to enclosure by private interests, as enabled by the British Enclosure Acts of the 18th and 19th century. Is there any sense in which the public goods of Wikipedia, open source software, and other enterprises of Creative Commons might be 'enclosed' for exploitation by the 'landlords' of digital infrastructure?

We might consider a case in which hundreds of people have dedicated a large amount of work to refining and crafting a specific Wikipedia page, creating an elegant and useful summary of, perhaps, the functioning of a vacuum cleaner. Now imagine that you have reason (perhaps while solving some small domestic crisis) to enter 'how does a vacuum cleaner work' into your search engine, which kindly refers you to the product resulting from the labour of all those people. In fact many search engines do not even direct you to Wikipedia – they insert the text you need right into the search results page – alongside advertisements for new vacuum cleaners. These are paid for by the manufacturers and directed to you as with any other advertising-funded content. Except that the revenue from this advertising does not go to the creators of the content, simply to the creator of the infrastructure that has delivered it. Whatever the motivations of the original authors, this public good has been 'enclosed' for profit, neither acknowledging their authorship nor seeking their permission.

One final reflection on the moral hazards of digital 'content' can be added to this awareness of the seconds and minutes of our lives that are spent attending, writing, and making decisions that are attributed to AI. Living as a human means constructing yourself as a person, becoming an individual and having agency over your own actions. These qualities of life are restricted or removed from workers in classical factories in ways that we are quite familiar with. However, we are less alert to the way they are being removed from us today. In particular, imagine if your personal history, your memories, and your relationships to all those around you, were owned by a company. These are the things that make us a person. And if personhood consists in your memories, your history and your friends, then the company who owns those things owns you as a person. The business models of 'social media' are nothing less than the commodification of personhood. This is a frightening prospect.

Winning the Turing Test

For many students of AI, the Turing Test is not only an interesting thought experiment for defining 'intelligence', but a challenge – a competition. They believe that they might 'win' the Turing test by making computers that are indistinguishable from humans – and indeed, there are competition prizes offered to those who might achieve that goal.

Computer science students, in particular, are fascinated by the idea of simulating human behaviour, and many of those who specialise in AI seek opportunities that would allow them to do so. When such students graduate, becoming the researchers and engineers who design new products for companies such as Google, Amazon or Facebook, those ambitions also seem to inspire the products and services being developed. Chatbot and 'voice assistant' products seem almost directly inspired by the Turing Test scenario, in a rare example of a philosophical proposition forming the basis for a successful business.

However, it is worth keeping in mind that there is more than one way to 'win' this competition, whose goal is to make it impossible to tell the difference between a computer and a human. In fact, there is a hard way and an easy way to 'win' the Turing test.

The hard way to 'win' the Turing test is to understand humans so thoroughly, and to be so expert in your construction of computer software, that you can make a computer so intelligent, versatile and sociable in its reasoning and conversation, that it is indistinguishable from a human.

The easy way to 'win' the Turing test is to make humans that are so stupid, so repetitive in their actions, so unoriginal, and so constrained in their capacity for emotional expression that they only distinguish between 'like' or indifference. Then you have 'won' by making humans as stupid as machines.

If the technologists who see the Turing test as a competition are given the opportunity to choose between these two alternatives, there seems a significant risk that we will drift toward the 'easy' option. In doing so, the risks of commodification, loss of personhood, enclosure of the commons, lack of authorial agency, and exploitation of attention become increasingly severe – because avoiding any of these requires close attention to the distinctions between human lives and abstract machines.

11

The Onward March of Commodification

Marx's Continuing Relevance for Understanding the Dynamics of 21st Century Capitalism

Ursula Huws

How Marxist theory deals with technology is a subject very close to my heart, given that I have been researching the impact of technology on employment and daily life for over 40 years. In my opinion, Marxist analysis has never been more relevant than now, in the second decade of the 21st century. People who feel that, somehow, technology has moved to a stage that can no longer be understood using the tools that Marx gave us (such as the labour theory of value) could not be more mistaken. The arguments used in these instances are arguments that Marx himself already anticipated and addressed in many cases.

Some of the current debates about the future reflect the rather strange and contradictory attitude to technology that Marxists have, an ambivalence that can actually be traced back to Marx himself. On the one hand there is a very clear understanding that capitalists use new technologies in order to cheapen and casualise labour, make workers more interchangeable with each other and bring in workers from the reserve army to substitute for organised workers. But on the other hand there is this idea that the bourgeoisie and capitalism have unleashed an enormous, unstoppable, creative-destructive wave of science which has the potential to take the drudgery out of work and to increase productivity in ways that could be socially beneficial. Certainly until the middle of the 20th century, most Marxists thought science and technology were synonymous with progress – with the idea that the forces of production had to be developed in order to create the basis for a socialist society. However I believe there was a little bit of a crisis in the mid-20th century in this way of thinking about technology. I am no expert in the history of public attitudes to technology but I suspect that the critical moment for a lot of people was the dropping of the atomic bomb on Hiroshima and Nagasaki, a moment when people suddenly became aware of the immense destructive power of new technologies produced by modern science.

This posed a fundamental challenge to the idea that technology was somehow neutral – something that could just be reappropriated, like the hammer that you can use to build a house with but also use to murder someone. The idea that technology could just be repurposed by socialists to do constructive things became increasingly problematic, partly because the technology became more sophisticated. Certainly from the 1970s onwards it became quite a generally held view among Marxists that the social relations of capitalism, in whatever current form, are actually, so to speak, designed into the technology. We cannot just reappropriate those technologies as they are; we have to think about how they can be redesigned and repurposed if we are to avoid repeating old patterns of domination and control.

The contradiction I mentioned earlier between these two different ideas of technology under capitalism – as an instrument of exploitation of labour on the one hand and as an instrument of liberation on the other – has underpinned a polarisation of views about the future of work. In one view you have utopian visions of a future, encompassed in the current jargon by phrases like 'the sharing economy', 'peer-to-peer networking' or the 'collaborative economy', as well as other examples. This is the idea that the technology we have can be repurposed to produce a kind of socialist utopia, with perhaps even no need for money, in which goods and services are freely exchanged, democratically. Opposed to this is a very dystopian view of a use of technology that reduces all workers to hyper-Taylorised, interchangeable units carrying out completely deskilled and boring work, ruled by algorithms. You can caricature the first position as leisure and freedom for all and a world in which we will only need to work a few hours a week because that is all you need for social production. And at the other extreme you have got the argument that the robots are going to take all the jobs, there is going to be mass unemployment and capitalism is going to be brought to its knees because robots do not buy cars.

It seems to me that both the utopian and dystopian scenarios are based on what is actually a rather similar set of assumptions, ones which Marx himself would have been among the first to challenge. They are generally based on a zero-sum idea of jobs – the idea that there are somehow a finite number of jobs around the world. These scenarios are also based on a view of the economy that only sees the paid tasks that are currently in the money economy, in the market and paid for. Thus all the tasks that are carried on outside the scope of capitalism as it now is, are seen as unpaid reproductive work and are rendered invisible and therefore not accounted for. This is similar to the utopian writing of the 1980s and 90s, with people like André Gorz and Ivan Illich writing about 'the end of the working class'. They basically added up all the hours that were currently worked, looked at the figures for productivity that were currently in the national statistics and divided these up by the size of the working population. And, lo and behold, they came to the conclusion that to enable everybody to have the basic necessities of life, people only have to work six hours a week in productive labour and the rest of their time can be devoted to creative and leisure activities. This leaves completely out of the picture the question of, while they are writing their symphonies: who is looking after the baby? Who is scrubbing the floor? Who is doing the cooking? Who is cleaning the toilet?

The history of capitalism's use of technology is not just a history of standardising and automating existing tasks, but is also a history of expansion and commodification, of bringing new activities within the scope of capitalist production. If you take a long historical look, you can see this broader pattern very clearly.

Typically it starts with a major economic crisis, a crisis of profitability for capitalists. A lot of capitalists go to the wall, but capitalism needs to expand, somehow. New capitalists come on the scene, with new business models that ignite a massive wave of restructuring. In that process, old industries shrink or die but very many new industries are born, and new technologies play a key role in this restructuring. After the crisis of the late 1920s for instance, we can see the way that the technology of electricity was used to bring into being all kinds of new machines that were basically substituting for what had been unpaid domestic labour, such as washing machines, vacuum cleaners, radios and so on. We can also learn from how the automobile industry grew in that period, substituting for the old service industries that involved looking after horses and similar tasks. Of course, lots of the jobs that involved looking after horses disappeared, but many more jobs were created in automobile factories.

Now, after the crisis of 2007/8, which we are living through right now, one can see precisely the same pattern. On the one hand, technologies such as robots, drones and 3D printers are being used to deskill what have in the past often been skilled jobs and make them more productive, getting rid of some jobs in the old rust-belt regions where workers have historically been well-organised. But we are also seeing the creation of many new jobs making drones and 3D printers; making the satellites that go up into space upon which all our supposedly immaterial communication relies; and making innumerable disposable junk objects such as mobile phone chargers and laptop cables that underpin the use of new information technology.

This is just one process that is going on, but more exist. We are also seeing an extension of capitalism into other areas of life that were previously outside the money economy, for example into art and culture where there is a huge wave of commodification going on. This can also be seen with nature, where we are seeing new bio-objects being created – new drugs being created by pharmaceutical companies for instance, as well as new products based on the patenting of DNA, new kinds of medical commodities and other developments.

Another vast new field of accumulation is the recommodification of that which was decommodified in the mid-20th century. A huge growth of public services took place as part of the post-war social democratic consensus that existed in most European countries, to some extent, and elsewhere in the world. Ten years ago in most OECD countries, public services represented around 46% of GDP; now it represents a huge new field of accumulation for capitalists. This started with the sale of council houses and nationalised industries, but the recommodification of public services moved beyond that. In some cases, it has taken place through the outsourcing of public services; in other cases through substituting private services for public ones as the latter are run down.

There is yet another enormous new field of accumulation for capital which I am currently researching, and that is the commodification of household labour. This is a topic which I think is very important if we are thinking seriously about strategies for women's liberation.

Marxist feminists have generally agreed that women cannot have genuine equality with men in our society until the 'burden of housework' (as it is often phrased) has been removed. Over the years there have been vigorous debates about how this can be achieved. Many first and second wave feminists argued that this should be done by socialising domestic labour. What we needed, they said, was public services like laundries, childcare, public restaurants and so on. Such demands made sense in that mid-20th century period when welfare states were growing. But in the 21st century, relying on that demand as a sole strategy is not terribly successful. First of all a lot of those services are being commodified – buying goods is replacing being provided with services. So for example, instead of having a mental health nurse you can have a psychotropic drug, which is a commodity produced by a drug company. Instead of having a public restaurant, you can buy a ready meal from Tesco. So that strategy of only demanding socialisation of domestic labour on its own becomes problematic. The alternative idea of providing wages for housework, promulgated by some radical feminists in the second wave, is problematic in a whole lot of other ways I will not go into now. And the idea (also put forward by some first and second wave feminists) that housework can just be automated out of existence is also problematic, for reasons I have written about elsewhere.

It seems to me that we have to look at the present situation in the context of the current restructuring of capitalism. Women have entered the workforce in unprecedented numbers in the last 30 years, which is partly connected with the cheapening value of wages and the fact that most workers need to live in two-worker households to have a decent standard of living. Women have only been able to enter the labour market on terms that are in any way equal with men through the labour of other women – a new servant class, made up especially of migrant women – who clean their houses and look after their kids and elderly dependants. Partly because of austerity policies, there has been a massive reduction in the public sector provision of these services. The private provision of these services has, up to now, largely taken place in the informal economy. In other words it has been what Marx would have called 'unproductive labour', which I would prefer to call 'reproductive labour' – labour that is paid for out of the wages of other workers and therefore is not producing surplus value for a capitalist. But what has happened in the last wave of restructuring is that much of this informal household labour has been sucked into the scope of global capitalism through online platforms like Taskrabbit, Deliveroo or Foodora. This is the first stage of a phenomenon that I believe will further advance.

We are in a stage now where the capitalists are using new technology to organise and discipline these workers and put them in touch with clients – but the business model is to take a rent, not to directly employ them. This, of course, is terribly reminiscent of the very early days of capitalism. The first factory owners did not employ the workers – they provided the space in which people could come and bring their own looms and from which the capitalists took a rent. So this is actually not a new pattern at all. This kind of platform capitalism is a transitional stage, I believe, because in the next stage the productivity of these workers will be increased by the use of more technology which will automate their work in various ways. It will replace goods for services, which is a classic capitalist plan. Uber, for example, is already, having got a near monopoly in taxi services in some US cities, investing in driverless cars. That is a capitalist strategy that I am sure Marx would have recognised as such. Now it is up to us to analyse this strategy and devise the means of combatting it.

12

Being a Marxist Artist Under Capitalism

Christine Lindey

How can Marxist artists put their beliefs and expertise at the service of socio-political struggle while working within a hostile, dominant aesthetic? This brief overview outlines courses of action taken in Mexico, the USA and Western Europe from the 1920s to the mid-1960s, by a few artists who exemplify a range of possible strategies. To avoid lengthy definitions of the term 'Marxist artist' I refer only to artists who self-identified as communists or as Marxists.

The lack of critical approval for socialist content and the ensuing paucity of patronage seriously hampered Marxist artists' economic survival and limited their access to the mass public they desired. Moreover many were professionally conflicted since they were educated and socialised under capitalism by successive dominant aesthetics, all rooted in early 19th century Romanticism. This defined artists as (male) special beings whose pursuit of originality and self-expression freed them from social responsibility. From the late 19th century onwards this was exacerbated by the influential 'art for art's sake' aesthetic, coupled with the rapid invention of successive modernist styles from Impressionism to Abstraction, which prioritised formal innovation over subject matter, thereby also freeing the content of art from social accountability. So Marxist artists were truly going against the grain, by creating socially useful art in accessible styles, which for most meant some form of 'realism'.

The carnage of WW1, the inspiration of the Bolshevik Revolution and the consequent growth of socialism elsewhere politicised many artists, as did the threat of nascent fascism. In the interwar years, impassioned debates about modernist versus realist styles became known as 'the battle of the styles'. Some of its complex intertwined threads raised the political issue of the social role of art. A major influence being the young Soviet Union's pluralist, socially inclusive cultural polices in which the vibrant avant-garde was energetically opposed by the Association of Artists for Revolutionary Russia (AKhRR). Founded in 1922 by young Marxists, they derided avant-garde 'abstract concoctions' and argued for an accessible, but forward look-ing realist art. Works such as Alexandr Deineka's absorbed moderate ele-ments of modernism in depictions of contemporary Soviet life during its revolutionary development. Western Marxists followed these ideas with great interest, and later the method of Socialist Realism announced in 1934.

As the domestic and international situation darkened after the 1929 Wall Street Crash, Marxists discussed how best to contribute to the urgent strug-gle against fascism. The most extreme and selfless course of action was to engage in direct action. The German artist Helmut Herzfelde had pre-empt-ed this as early as the First World War by taking the radical and dangerous act of anglicising his name to John Heartfield, in protest at the rabid nation-alist propaganda used to justify the war's mass slaughter, and in interna-tionalist solidarity with the 'enemy'. In the interwar years several artists took the equally radical step of giving up making art for full time political activism, for example by the Mexican David Siqueiros from 1925-1930 and the British Clive Branson from 1932-7.

Like several other artists they both also joined the International Brigades in the Spanish Republic, as did the British artist Felicia Browne. When her fellow artist Elizabeth Watson accused her of evading her commitment to her art Browne replied: '...I can only make out of what is valid or urgent to me. If painting or sculpture were more valid or urgent to me than the earthquake which is happening in the revolution... I should paint or make sculpture...'[1] She was the first British volunteer killed in action.

Others including John Heartfield in Germany and James Boswell, a New Zealander active in Britain, believed that they could be more politically use-ful by turning to agitational art. They gave up the critically more prestigious 'fine art', arguing that its unique works were exchangeable commodities which pandered to bourgeois acquisitiveness and elitism; whereas ephem-eral posters, cartoons, leaflets, placards and decorated floats were public arts, through which to propagate socialism. Boswell's illustrations in Brit-ain's *Left Review* and Heartfield's photomontages in Germany's *AIZ* sati-rised and exposed ruling class privilege, indicted social immiseration and injustice, and exposed the war-mongering and profiteering which spurred the fascist destruction in Spain.

Both artists' works absorbed aspects of avant-garde innovations while remaining visually accessible. Boswell's illustrations satirised ruling class mannerisms and posturing through Expressionist distortions and acute line. Heartfield's photomontages juxtaposed disparate imagery to expose fascist savagery, as in 'This is the salvation which they bring' (1938), in which the

X-ray photograph of a hand transmutes the skeletal fingers into the smoke trails of the warplanes which destroyed the cadavers and ruined buildings below.

Agitational art was vital to the political struggle but it differed patently in form and function from self-generated art. One requires speed of understanding of focused, topical messages, whereas the other permits more contemplative responses to multivalent, elliptical appeals to the emotions, the psyche and the intellect. Many artists such as the British Priscilla Thornycroft and Cliff Rowe produced both.

The dream for Western artists was to create permanent public art via sculptures and murals through which to convey multivalent Marxist ideas and narratives. But this, of course, depended on public patronage. This was briefly achieved in the 1920s by Mexican revolutionary artists led by Diego Riviera, José Orozco and David Siqueurios who formed the Syndicate of Technical Workers, Painters and Sculptors in 1922. Its manifesto denounced easel painting and called for collectives of waged artists to create a monumental public art to celebrate the national identify of the native Mexican people. They persuaded the progressive Secretary of State José Vasconcelos (1921-1924), who was committed to artistic freedom, to commission public murals. Some of their murals criticised capitalism, celebrated socialism and honoured the native peoples and their hitherto disparaged cultures, including by drawing upon their visual traditions.

This state patronage was quickly withdrawn but meanwhile Marxists including Pablo O'Higgins formed the collective Taller de Gráfica Popular (People's Graphic Workshop) to defend and enrich the native peoples' culture, propagate socialism and reflect the social reality of their times. Their 'street art' resonated with the largely illiterate or semi-literate population who were familiar with the popular print tradition of pictorial song and news sheets. Unlike the muralists, the printmakers were not reliant on state funding or on access to public sites so they continued to be active into the 1960s.

The Mexican muralists and printmakers were influential in the USA. Several American printmaking collectives sprang up and Americans formed an Artists Union in 1933. Mexican artists also got mural commissions in the USA, the most famous and notorious ones being by Rivera. They were sometimes assisted by young Americans. When Siqueurios established his Experimental Workshop in New York, the young socialist Jackson Pollock worked on their imaginative kinetic floats for the Communist Party USA.

During Roosevelt's New Deal Public Works Arts Projects (c.1933-1943), approximately 2,500 murals for public buildings were commissioned by US Federal and State governments, partly influenced by the Mexican muralists. Some were by Marxists, such as William Gropper's *Construction of the Dam* (1938). His mural's clarity of content, accessible realist style and celebration of the heroism of dangerous and inventive labour, could well have been painted in the USSR. Yet its context in Washington's Department of the Interior, a major Federal State building, made its content radical and highly controversial. Not only was it publicly commissioned and financed, but it celebrated the rare creation of a publicly funded major power supply in capitalist America, where private ownership of services was the norm. New Deal art in general was heavily criticised as a 'socialistic' waste of public funds by powerful right wing Senators and Congressmen and it was soon phased out.

For most Western Marxists, lack of public patronage meant that mural commissions had to remain a dream, yet artists' desire to express themselves fully via fine art persisted. But rather than focusing on formal experimentation and/or individualistic content they created socially committed content in accessible styles, which exposed them to accusations of rear-guard traditionalism, irrelevant to modern times. This situation was exacerbated during the first phase of the Cold War by dominant American critics who raised Abstract Expressionism to the pinnacle of 'international' high art; thereby further demonising Soviet Socialist Realism, and by association Western realisms, especially socially committed ones.

Yet some Western Marxists doggedly ploughed this lonely furrow in the late 1940s and 1950s. Their styles varied from the precise realism of the African-American Charles White, to the legible but simplified forms and outlines of the British Cliff Rowe and the American Alice Neel, to the Cubo-Expressionism of the French Fernand Léger, the Italian Renato Guttuso and the British-Genoese Peter de Francia.

Their works honoured the lives and struggles of those who produce the means of life. For example White, Guttuso, Léger, and Rowe depicted the social importance of labour in fields, factories and building sites. Neel painted non-commissioned portraits from life, of people she knew: her neighbours in Manhattan's Spanish Harlem, her left-wing comrades or people she met by chance. Portraits such as the *Daily Worker* reporter, Art Shields (1951) or the taxi driver, Abdul Rahman, (1964) reveal her sitters' essential character with respect, empathy and psychological insight. Taken as a whole, Neel's numerous portraits provide a lasting testament to the social value, spirit and resilience of the American working-class.

The most problematic course of action during the Cold War was to create non-commissioned political art, since the lack of access to a wide public defeated the works' immediate political purpose. Moreover, political narratives meant turning to the long-discredited genre of history painting. Although this resulted in widespread self-censorship, some Marxists persisted. In the 1950s Peter de Francia painted three large history paintings to express his outrage at current political injustices. The last of these, 'The Bombing of Sakiet' (1959), is an angry indictment of the French air force's bombing of the defenceless Tunisian village during the Algerian War of Independence, on the pretext that it harboured Algerian 'terrorists'. Painted in a legible Cubo-Expressionist style its emotive anti-war and anti-imperialist content later eclipsed its topicality to achieve a universality which sadly, is all too pertinent in our own times.

The most famous Marxist artist is Picasso. He was already middle-aged and internationally famous as a pioneer of the avant-garde, when he was politicised by the Spanish Civil War. His *Guernica* (1937) remains arguably the most famous and powerful political painting. He formally became a Marxist in 1944 when he joined the French Communist Party (PCF). Yet he painted very few overtly political paintings such as *Massacre in Korea* (1951). Caught in the cross-fire of the cultural Cold War, his political allegiance was to the PCF but his aesthetic allegiance was to the Modernism which he had pioneered. Picasso claimed artistic freedom saying: '... I am a Communist and my painting is Communist painting ... But if I were a shoemaker, Royalist or Communist or anything else, I would not necessarily hammer my shoes in a special way to show my politics...'[2] Yet his works were always figurative rather than abstract, they radiated a love of humanity, and he unstintingly contributed designs to *L'Humanité* and for communist events such as his Dove of Peace on posters for the Communist Peace Congresses of 1949, 1950, and 1952.

But Picasso's main course of action as a communist artist was to use his fortune and international celebrity status for the movement. He lent his name to numerous national and international political causes and campaigns and gave them enormous sums of money, for example giving one million francs to the French Miners' Support Fund during the 1947-8 strikes.

The work of less famous Marxists were mostly ignored or marginalised by mainstream critics, curators and art historians. But they were exhibited and reproduced by small, underfunded left-wing publications and organisations, and a few were discovered by the mainstream decades later. Neel, who had survived as a single parent on welfare in the slums of Spanish Harlem for most of her adult life, eventually achieved critical success in her seventies due to the support of the socialist feminist art historian Linda Nochlin, and others. In 2016 the Tate Gallery belatedly bought de Francia's history painting *The Execution of Beloyannis* (1953), which exposed the brutal injustices of the Greek dictatorship, half a century after the outrage and four years after the artist's death.

Marxist artists struggled with the dilemmas of reconciling their commitment to political change with their socialised expectation of total artistic freedom. Janos, the artist protagonist in John Berger's 1958 novel *A Painter of Our Time*, concluded that the artist must be free, but the work 'must be judged in relation to the always different and always present struggle of men [sic] to realise their potentiality more fully...'[3]

Taking diverse courses of action, all Marxist artists under capitalism courageously stuck to their convictions despite most of them suffering critical obscurity. Their agitational works made vital contributions to political and social campaigns and their self-directed works kept alive the flame of social-ist art which they passed on to the newly politicised young artists of the late 1960s and 1970s.

NOTES

1   F. Browne, cited in S. Martin, *Conscience and Conflict, British Artists and the Spanish Civil War* (Pallant House Gallery, 2014), pp. 40-41.

2   D. Ashton, *Picasso on Art: A Selection of View*s (London and New York, Thames and Hudson, 1972), p. 140.

3   J. Berger, *A Painter of Our Time* (Harmondsworth, Secker and Warburg/ Penguin Books, 1958 /1965), p. 61.

13

Literature and Political Judgment

David Margolies

Marx, in his *Thesis XI on Feuerbach*, said: 'Philosophers have only interpreted the world in various ways; the point, however, is to change it.' Too often Marxists have taken a narrow view of how change can be produced and have thought of literature either as publications the 'lit. sec'. sells to comrades or, if we are considering imaginative literature, as a mere pastime. We know that politics extends into all areas of life – the personal is still political – and literature, even if it is seen as only entertainment, can have, does have, a political effect.

The question really is what does it mean that 'literature is political' and how can literature play a positive political role? At the simplest level it is sometimes assumed that readers presented with a good political perspective will be moved to the left. But political responses are much more complicated than that; people's reasons for, say, voting in a particular way, derive from a range of factors which include many diverse things. Their views may mirror what is presented in the mass media, may conform to the opinions of their friends, may be a response to Facebook and Twitter communications and be influenced by a wide range of individual experience and personal history. The point is that their views and actions result from processes that are very complex, in which their class position is only one factor. To expect a working-class person to vote Labour because they are told that Labour stands 'for the many, not the few' is simplistic and it is politically inadequate. We have to recognise that to overcome the media's constant rubbishing of left-wing values and their consolidated campaign against Labour, we often have to start slowly; that is, we have to begin not with a vision of the socialist society we want – in the popular view socialism cannot work and should be rejected – but with material concerns of everyday life: for example, housing and education. It should not be the question of whether or not they can be afforded by our society but whether, as part of society, it should be recognised as a right. Thatcher's most characteristic statement was 'There is no such thing as society; only individuals and their families'. Her most enduring negative achievement was to establish individualist thinking, personal advantage rather than social benefit: 'my car, my child, my flat' (previously Council flat). Overcoming that belief that everything starts with the individual is a fundamental political task; we must persuade people to be willing to consider things from a social perspective. The first element of such persuasion is to recognise that people who say things that are reactionary are not necessarily inherently hostile; they may have concerns where they would be able to recognise that a social solution is necessary. This gives them the potential to be politically positive. People's choices are complex. This is not wishy-washy liberalism; it is thinking dialectically, part of the heritage of Marx.

I want to look at two examples of literature in terms of how a political attitude may be encouraged in a process that seems not at all political. The first is a short fiction, one of the most popular works of its day but little known now and not well regarded in English departments – Robert Greene's *Pandosto* (1584). It has not quite disappeared from English studies because Shakespeare made heavy use of it in *The Winter's Tale* and also has echoes of it in *The Tempest*. The plot is constructed out of traditional, folkloric themes – a royal baby set adrift in a little boat, found by a shepherd looking for a lost sheep, raised in poverty to be a shepherdess with no awareness of her origins and then courted by a prince. The proposed cross-class relationship is a central issue. The social order that prevailed when Greene wrote accepted hierarchy as a fundamental principle. Those who over-reached could expect to fall. This is what was taught by the Church and echoed in much of the culture of the time, and Greene pays lip-service to it. Fawnia, the foundling heroine, tells the prince that they cannot marry, that everything is against it. But then she adduces some counter-arguments from Greek mythology – that love is a god that cannot be resisted, and the couple elope. They are caught, but escape punishment because the old shepherd produces the jewellery he found with the baby and had hidden, which shows her to be a princess. Thus there is no longer a class barrier and prince and re-discovered princess are married.

The standard critical argument in regard to *Pandosto* is that hierarchy was not actually violated, and for that reason the action is acceptable. The story thus is regarded as confirming the status quo and the importance of hierarchy. But in most of the book Greene treats Fawnia's peasant status as the reality and the social disparity is accepted as real (there aren't any intrusive hints that Fawnia is actually a princess). The prince, Dorastus, is unwilling to accept Fawnia's resistance and will use his rank to enforce his desire: 'thou must needs yield, for thou knowest I can command and constrain'. She replies 'but not to love, for constrained love is force, not love'. She can love him, she says, 'when Dorastus becomes a shepherd'. Greene then moves to a comic turn when Dorastus arrives in a shepherd's outfit, announcing that he has made the change required to win her love. Fawnia answers with a wit that is both popular and literary (it sends up pastoral conventions): 'Shepherds are not called shepherds because they wear hooks and bags but that they are born poor and live to keep sheep. So this attire hath not made Dorastus a shepherd, but to seem like a shepherd'. Their subsequent actions when Fawnia has accepted Dorastus, are carried out in full consciousness that they are rejecting convention and the authority of the hierarchy.

Although the plot in fact suggests acceptance of convention because the happy ending depends on convention having been followed in substance, Greene's challenge to hierarchy is not through the plot. Plot is the vehicle, not the centre of the story; it is not what Greene enlivens in the fiction by giving it development. Rather what is given most consideration is the motives of the characters, on which the action depends. The emphasis on character and motive focuses the story at the level of reader experience. That is, although the plot is, frankly, ridiculous, the behaviour of the principal characters is recognisable as anchored in real-life considerations. Fawnia is far and away the most important character, not only in terms of the narrative space she occupies, but also in being the person who must weigh situations and make the important decisions. Greene is making a double challenge here: he gives a woman the most important role (as he does in almost all his extensive fiction), and Fawnia's viewpoint is the perspective in which the action is presented. She weighs the arguments of social propriety against her own will, and it is her will that determines the action. Greene is thereby validating individual judgement over convention, as well as recognising gender equality (he was referred to by Thomas Nashe as 'the Homer of women').

Of course the characters of *Pandosto* exist only in a fictional world, but a world that nevertheless reflects the social order of the real world in which Greene's readers live. The arguments for individual choice are powerful and, most importantly, they are transferable. The persuasiveness comes not from information but from attitude; Greene provides a context that justifies individualism. In effect he helps to alter the emotional balance of social conformity and individual will. Instead of individualism being a cause of guilt, something seen as functionally anti-social, Greene provides the bourgeois with a social entitlement for his individualism.

I feel it is important to stress that Greene's 'justification' is not a rational argument, and readers who expect political persuasion to occur primarily through reasoning usually fail to recognise that Greene could serve a potentially political function. And this is the point about political judgement that

I would like to make – it is not usually dependent on explicit political positions. Marx admired Balzac, despite his conservatism, for the understanding of the mechanics of French bourgeois society displayed in his novels. That is largely concerned with rational understanding. Perhaps more to the point, Gramsci wrote about working-class admiration for the newspaper serialised version of *The Man in the Iron Mask* and said it is not based on the hero's aristocratic status but on his fighting injustice, a struggle with which they can identify. What is important, what I am concerned with, is not a work's information but its power to affect readers' orientation.

I want to take my second example from children's books. They are particularly good material for showing the shaping of attitude because their models of behaviour are unusually clear and modern ones are seldom constructed primarily to impart knowledge. Yet many people, even radicals attuned to distinctions of ideology, tend to regard them as unimportant. They may recognise the value of time spent reading to a child but are still indifferent to the values put forward in the books and do not regard the choice of book as a matter of concern. The very nature of fiction is to create imagined people and situations, and, however fanciful, they bear a relation to behaviour that occurs in the real world. In effect they test modes of behaviour; to read them is to experiment in what it means to behave in different ways. And because children's experience of the world is necessarily limited, the models in fiction are likely to have a greater effect than they would for an adult.

I will illustrate from personal experience. When one of our daughters, aged about three or four, came home from play group, she was talking to me in the kitchen while I was preparing supper. She asked if our friend Rick was married. When I said 'no', her response was, 'Poor Rick, he's got no one to cook his supper'. Where had she acquired this notion of gender roles? Certainly not at home! The stories in the playgroup mirrored the gender distinctions of the dominant ideology.

The children's book I want to look at is one that is very well known – Maurice Sendak's *Where the Wild Things Are* (1963). Sendak drew the illustrations as well as writing the story. They have realistic elements of architecture and decor but more to give a sense of what they represent rather than provide any hint of photographic realism. The colours are muted, giving an impression rather than a sharp sense of material reality, and the textures of furnishings and the environment are done in pen-and-ink patterning that makes more prominent awareness that these are drawings. The effect is of something real-ish rather than real.

Max is about six years old and in the beginning of the book is a terror: 'The night Max wore his wolf suit and made mischief of one kind and another'. This involved behaviour that was clearly unacceptable in the domestic context – hammering nails into the wall and terrifying the dog. 'His mother called him 'WILD THING!' and Max said 'I'LL EAT YOU UP!' so he was sent to bed without eating anything'. The illustrations show a child in a tantrum – angry but also finding satisfaction in being an irritation in his ordered world. In traditional fashion he is punished with a partial exclusion from that world, being sent to bed without supper. In his attitude of resentment he shows resistance – he has not abandoned his tantrum mood, his individualism is still holding out against accepting social judgement of his behaviour.

He then enters into the dream world: 'that very night in Max's room a forest grew and grew – and grew until his ceiling hung with vines/ and the walls became the world all around/ and an ocean tumbled by with a private boat for Max/ and he sailed off through night and day and in and out of weeks/ and almost over a year/ to where the wild things are'. The blending of time and space (sailing in and out of weeks) emphasises the location in imagination. The wild things are drawn to look a bit like medieval depictions of devils but they retain the rounded character of illustrations for children. 'They roared their terrible roars and gnashed their terrible teeth/ and rolled their terrible eyes and showed their terrible claws', but Max tames them 'with the magic trick/ of staring into all their yellow eyes without blinking once' and they 'made him king of all wild things'.

Sendak then has Max say, 'let the wild rumpus start!' and the creatures, part recognisable animal but fantastically fierce with their large claws and horns, all jump up and down. They look quite dangerous but also have a playfulness that makes them less scary, even somewhat attractive. The 'wild rumpus' goes on for six pages – no text; all illustration – until, "Now stop!' Max said and sent the wild things off to bed/ without their supper. And Max the king of all wild things was lonely/ and wanted to be where someone loved him best of all'. The reality of his bedroom intrudes as smell: 'Then all around from far away across the world/ he smelled good things to eat/ so he gave up being king of where the wild things are'. The wild things plead with him not to leave but Max waves good-bye 'and sailed back over a year/ and in and out of weeks/ and through a day and into the night of his very own room/ where he found his supper waiting for him/ and it was still hot'.

Clearly the story does not have a political content but it has attitudes that are important. Max's display of frustrations and anger as an individual alienates him from his surrounding society in the household. But in going where the wild things are, exorcising his tantrum, he realises he wants social reintegration – to be where someone loves him. The point of the story ('point' is really too specific – Sendak does not provide for an articulated conclusion), is that social integration is positive. This sense is created as much or perhaps more by the illustrations. The story recognises that individuals sometimes experience explosions of temper, but that can be tolerated if they exist in an environment where return to the social is possible. In an environment such as we have today, more and more individualistic, anything that strengthens social feeling is positive simply in terms of inter-change with other people. But it is also politically positive in that people must feel that social being is fundamental if we want to build socialism. Thatcher managed to establish for much of the country that individualism was the normal way to be. In *Where the Wild Things Are*, for Sendak, social beings are what is normal. It is an excellent argument that a political effect can be achieved by non-political, artistic means.

In regard to literature, I think that Marx teaches us that we must recog-nise that it has effects that can be understood as political – political in the sense that all imaginative reconstructions and organisations of experience involve principles of social being. It follows that political judgement is ap-propriate. But we should also recognise that this does not mean imposing a line on literature. This kind of control was tried under the guise of social-ist realism with negative results. It was demanded of authors that, in ef-fect, they showed positive political results; works that simply showed the process of politicisation were judged inadequate. Literature can be part of changing the world, and we can criticise it from that perspective, but to do so usefully, we must recognise that people and human processes are highly complex.

14

The Ecological Marx?

Ted Benton

Introduction

clearly remember preparing to teach Marx to undergraduates, and having to trawl through the literature on 'alienation', and then re-reading the *Economic and Philosophical Manuscripts* of 1844. Alienation, everyone said, was about the relationship between capital and labour, alienation from the worker's life-activity, from the process and product of that activity, and from his or her fellow workers. No-one seemed to have noticed that for Marx the most fundamental source of all other dimensions of alienation was alienation from nature, and that, for him at that time, communism was a vision of reconciliation among humans on the basis of reconciliation with nature:

> '…it is the genuine resolution of the conflict between man and nature and man and man.' (Marx 1967a, p. 95)

This tendency to marginalise the significance of nature in Marx's thinking has been dominant in much secondary literature, and in the politics of those who have drawn inspiration from Marx's ideas. The rise to prominence of green politics and the 1970s and 1980s appeared initially as a challenge not only to existing political and economic institutions, but also to Marxists and large parts of the non-Marxist left. Here was what could be understood as a potentially catastrophic consequence of capitalist 'development' that was hardly on the left's agenda. The vision of a politics that was both red and green emerged out of this, and it involved, among other things, rejecting the claim that greens often made at that time, that environmental politics were 'beyond left and right'. However, it also meant a critical re-think of much of the legacy of the left. This was in part a work of rediscovery. How could William Morris have been a Marxist, yet also the author of *News from Nowhere*, a utopian novel that puts the transformation of our relation to nature at the centre of its vision? Several key thinkers in the Frankfurt School of Critical Theory, most notably Marcuse, had recognised the fatefully destructive forces of capitalist 'modernity', and there were other, less recognised thinkers who had long ago followed this line of thinking. In 1989 I published a piece in *New Left Review*, taking the questioning to Marx's own work. I opened the argument by recognising the commonality between Marx and green thinking, but went on to explore the sources in Marx's writings for non-green, even anti-green, readings that had been so influential on the left, concluding with evidence of the possibility of quite alternative interpretations. Some more 'orthodox' Marxists read my work as a critique of Marx, rather than a critique *of some readings* of Marx, and an attempt to develop a largely unexplored ecological dimension to his work. Meanwhile, several scholars in the US and elsewhere were developing interpretations of Marx that recognised him as 'ecological' all along.

Since then, writers who work within the broad tradition of historical materialism have been, to a degree, divided between those who draw more-or-less exclusively from Marx, or Marx and Engels, for their theoretical orientation, and others who are committed to some re-thinking or development of the core ideas of the tradition, often combining them with independent sources of inspiration.

Marx's legacy

Since we are celebrating the 200th anniversary of Marx's birth, I will focus firstly on his legacy, before considering later developments in ecological Marxism. I will do this by commenting briefly on what we can take from four 'staging posts' in Marx's life-work, starting with the *Economic and Philosophical Manuscripts of 1844* (Marx 1967a). As I have already noted, Marx's central theme is a philosophical account of history as a double process of social division and estrangement from nature as a result of private property. The conflict between owners and workers will eventually lead to a classless society of associated producers who are reconciled with the rest of nature. This future state is one in which the human 'species-being' is realised and humanism become naturalism. Many striking passages assert humans' continual dependence on interaction with nature for their lives, human commonality with animals as 'active natural beings', humans as 'part of nature', and linked to nature not just for food and shelter, but also for 'spiritual nourishment'. This is a non-reductive naturalistic view of humans and our dependency on nature which is indispensable for any serious green philosophy. However, there are some ambiguities. Although Marx sees a commonality between humans and animals, as 'active natural beings', he also strongly contrasts human and animal beings, sometimes representing the degraded state of alienated human life as equivalent to animal existence. Marx's way of thinking about the realisation of our 'species being' as a process of collective, creative work on nature as 'humanisation of nature' is also open to many interpretations. Does the 'humanisation of nature' leave space for wild nature, or for other species whose lives are lived independently of ours? What would be left of nature as 'other', not in the sense of estrangement, but as object of awe, curiosity and delight? As it happens, the *Manuscripts* are alive with comments that show Marx's recognition of these dimensions of an emancipated relation to nature (not least his reference to nature as 'spiritual nourishment'). The *Manuscripts* were private expressions of the thoughts of one of the greatest thinkers of modern times at a particular moment. They are not a finished body of thought, but they do offer some key ideas for confronting our own predicaments.

Only three or four years later, Marx had joined with Engels in composing their most widely read intervention: the *Communist Manifesto* of 1848 (Marx & Engels 1967). By this time, Engels had written what must be the founding work of the ecological justice movement, demonstrating the environmental degradation and unhealthy conditions of working-class families in the great industrial cities – class injustices reached out beyond the factory to infect every aspect of working-class life (Engels 1969). But the *Manifesto* conveys also a sense of excited wonderment at the forces unleashed by modern industrial capitalism. After a brief sketch of history as a succession of modes of production, each with its distinctive form of class conflict, they hail the immense transformative power of the current, bourgeois phase of historical development in this astonishing passage:

> 'The bourgeoisie, during its rule of scarce 100 years, has created more massive and more colossal productive forces than have all preceding generations together. Subjection of Nature's forces to man, machinery, application of chemistry to industry and agriculture, steam-navigation, railways, electric telegraphs, clearing of whole continents for cultivation, canalization of rivers, whole populations conjured out of the ground – what earlier century had even a presentiment that such productive forces slumbered in the lap of social labour?' (Marx & Engels 1967, p. 85)

This apparent celebration of the development of the forces for transformation of nature by the modern capitalist class, together with Marx's view that these forces will eventually need to be liberated as they become restrained by capitalist relations, have been read by some as indicating Marx's 'promethean' view of history. On this account, Marx is committed to the ever-expanding domination of nature, subjecting it to human purposes even under the future communist society, but that state being distinguished by the fruits of that mastery being evenly shared.

That radically anti-ecological interpretation is challenged by John Bellamy Foster, one of the most rigorous and scholarly of the defenders of 'Marx's ecology', especially in his book of that title (Foster 2000). He notes that other commentators have seen Marx and Engels's apparent commitment to the subjection of nature, industrialisation of agriculture, clearing of whole continents for cultivation and so on have seen this as paying insufficient attention to sustainability. Foster's response is to point out that subjection of nature might be interpreted in Baconian terms as necessarily obeying nature in order to 'command her', and also that Marx and Engels might have been recognising the positive achievement of 'pushing back' famine. But, Foster comments,

> 'it did point to the fact that the preservation of wilderness was not Marx and Engels's prime concern.' (ibid., p. 139)

Of course, these statements from Marx and Engels did more than show that wilderness preservation was not a prime concern for them at that time – on the face of it, they suggest such concerns were completely absent. Foster was probably here having a dig against a certain US strand of 'deep ecology', but the easy dismissal of concern for wilderness, or wild nature, does indicate something about Bellamy Foster's version of ecological Marxism.

If what I have presented as the second 'staging post' in Marx's thinking can easily be read as an endorsement of industrial capitalism's immense dynamism in harnessing the forces of nature, from a different normative perspective it can be read as a powerful account of the intrinsic connection between capitalist development and the domination of nature – a crucial corrective to environmental philosophies in our own time that attribute ecological destruction to human nature, technology, population growth, consumer choice and the rest.

The third 'staging post' is the astonishingly condensed account of Marx's theoretical frame for thinking about human history that he gives in his Preface to *A Contribution to the Critique of Political Economy* (the '1859 Preface', Marx 1971). This 'guiding thread' for historical study includes the familiar succession of 'modes of production' from ancient through feudal to 'modern bourgeois', and with the Asiatic mode as brief acknowledgement of non-Western forms. The key dynamic of historical transformation derives from conflicts developing within each mode between 'material forces' of production and the social relations (property relations, relations of domination, class relations) of production whose character defines each distinct mode.

Even in this highly schematic form, these ideas have a fundamental bearing on our understanding of the relation between human societies and (the rest of) nature. In this respect, there are three main achievements. First, the key to understanding the distinctive character of any society, its internal patterns of conflict, and its dynamic tendencies is the structure of relations through which human labour is combined to work upon nature in the meeting of need, and how the product of that labour is distributed to people who stand in the different positions defined by that structure of relations. In other words, the specific ways in which a society manages its need-meeting interaction with nature are crucial to understanding the whole society, and its prospects. This is why the tradition of thinking established by Marx is directly open to an understanding of the ecological conditions and transactions between societies and nature. In contrast, this has proved difficult if not impossible for subsequent traditions of social theory that are grounded in dualistic oppositions between nature and society, nature and culture, and animal and human (see, for example, Benton 1977, 2015).

The second respect in which these ideas offer illumination for our current situation is that they undercut any attempt to consider human ecology independently of reference to the distinctive character of a mode of production. Each distinct pattern of property relations, form of subordination of labour, combination of materials in use, employment of technology, source of power, and so on, has its own ecology: its own particular set of ecological conditions of possibility, and its own distinctive scale and types of impact on the rest of nature. This frame of thought, then, adds further depth and elaboration to the insight derived from the *Communist Manifesto*: the ecological predicament of modern capitalism is just that – not a consequence of greed, population, consumer choice, competition, or even economic growth – except and unless understood as aspects of a specifically capitalist social and economic order.

And what of the third insight? Marx's education in Hegelian philosophy left him predisposed to understand transformation in terms of contradiction, or in his transformed version, in terms of structurally produced social antagonisms between rival class formations, one striving to hold on to its ascendancy, the other struggling to bring into being a new, more historically progressive order. We might well (as I am) be sceptical of Marx's particular understanding of the simplification of class relations in advanced capitalism, and his expectation of universal proletarian revolution. However, and again this signals the advantages of historical materialism over almost all other approaches, Marx was right to identify inherent contradictions in specifically capitalist political economies, and to draw out the consequences of these for broad patterns of social conflict and resistance. Ecological politics needs – and indeed has – persuasive arguments, well-grounded in rigorously produced evidence, but these will not be acted upon, or hardly heard, unless powerful and challenging social movements for radical transformation propound them. While many environmental organisations appeal to business and government with their talk of 'natural capital', 'ecosystem services' and cost/ benefit analysis, the alarming evidence from the most recent report of the IPCC about the radical changes needed to avoid runaway climate change disappeared from public discourse within 24 hours.

So, now onto the fourth 'staging post'. This is the culmination of Marx's intellectual struggles – his major critical analysis of the capitalist mode of production, distribution and exchange. Marx's *Capital* (subtitled in English translation, as *A Critical Analysis of Capitalist Production*) was not completed in his lifetime, but has nevertheless been, rightly, treated as his major intellectual achievement. From the point of view of our theme here, perhaps the key feature of Marx's argument is his distinction between, on one side, the 'concrete' labour process, involving distinct skills, deployments of energy and materials etc., and resulting in a product with characteristics that make it an object of human use – its use-value, and, on the other, the 'production process', according to which raw materials, means of production and human labour power are combined to produce a commodity with a definite value in exchange with other commodities. The logic of the production process is the delivery of a surplus in exchange value over the exchange-value of the inputs into the process (in Marx's view, the latter resolving into the exchange value of labour power – leaving aside the complex question of the role of monopoly rent). The term 'logic' is appropriate here, since the calculations that are determinant in commodity production are formally rational and abstract – all the rich qualitative diversity of things, resources, activities, processes and means that enter into the labour process is reduced to the single dimension of monetary calculation. Once an economic system operates by way of independent units of production, each producing commodities for exchange on the market, according to a single measure of value (exchange value), the system is necessarily dominated by competitive accumulation, and the abstract logic that drives it.

However, the abstract form of commodity production coexists in the same complex system as the concrete labour process – it is the abstract logic that drives the assemblage and coordination of materials, sources of energy, combinations of workers with their various skills and aptitudes, and so on. The formation and direction of the labour process is subject to the formal logic of commodity production, but at the same time, commodity production cannot occur independently of its harnessing of the labour process to provide it with saleable use values. As is well-known, Marx's analysis of the production process shows it to be inherently exploitative of the wage-workers, whose capacity for labour is put to work by the capitalist under conditions which allow the latter to appropriate a value greater than the (exchange) value laid out. Since it is the activity of the labourer that makes the difference between a set of inert implements, materials etc., and a product, the key ratio is that of the outlay on the worker's labour (the wage) and the surplus (profit) over total outlay. Exploitation by capital over labour is thus, for Marx, intrinsic to capitalist production, not some ethical failing of particular employers. The working through of this core contradiction at the heart of capitalist production provided Marx with his explanatory theory of the dynamic of class struggle as the main vehicle for the overthrow of capitalism and the emergence of a new epoch. It is therefore understandable that these relations are the main focus of his analysis in *Capital*.

However, the distinction between the concrete labour process and the abstract process of production of commodity value can also be used as a frame for analysing the sources of ecological degradation and destruction specific to capitalism. One way of showing this is to recognise that many of the conditions and consequences of the expansionary dynamic of capitalist production are either imperceptible or a matter of indifference from the standpoint of the overriding logic of abstract costs and benefits. The tendency of the system will be to overuse whatever comes as a 'free gift of nature', while potentially toxic emissions are offloaded to others ('externalities') and labour is exploited without reference to its social, psychological or physiological conditions for reproduction. These are, of course, tendencies – they do not run their full course, or the system would dissolve in its own social and ecological contradictions in very short order. So what sets limit to these tendencies? Does whatever that is itself act without limit? I will come back to these questions.

The 'ecological Marx'

Meanwhile, it should be noted that Marx himself, though writing long before the global existential threat posed by the current phase of capitalist 'development', had already begun to work out some of these implications. Relatively recent scholarship, notably conducted by Foster and Paul Burkett in the course of their recovery and defence of an ecological Marx, shows the importance of Marx's interest in agriculture during the period of his work towards the writing of *Capital*. A crisis of declining soil fertility in the early decades of the 19th century had led to a global search for fertilizer, in human bones from battlefields to guano from Peru. In 1837 the chemist Justus von Liebig was commissioned by the Royal Society to produce a work on chemistry as applied to agriculture. His *Agricultural Chemistry* of 1840 showed the necessity of nitrogen, phosphorus and potassium for plant growth. Difficulties in replacing all these requirements for plant nutrition led Liebig to shift perspective from attempts to replace lost soil fertility towards a critique of capitalist agriculture. As Foster shows, Marx followed this literature closely and saw the relationship between the loss of soil fertility as endemic to capitalist agriculture and the urban problems of waste disposal and pollution (as analysed by Engels many years before). The separation of town and country resulted in the depletion of soil fertility as agricultural produce was exported to urban centres, so that waste was not returned to the soil as organic fertilizer, but, instead, ended up as environmental pollution in the towns and cities.

Marx explains this in a section of *Capital* on the relation between modern industry and agriculture. Capitalist development, he argues, has driven peasant farmers from the land, concentrating them in the towns as wage-labourers. At the same time:

> '...it disturbs the circulation of matter between matter and the soil, i.e. prevents the return to the soil of its elements consumed by man in the form of food and clothing; it therefore violates the conditions necessary to the lasting fertility of the soil. By this action it destroys at the same time the health of the town labourer and the intellectual life of the rural labourer. But while upsetting the naturally grown conditions for the maintenance of that circulation of matter, it imperiously calls for its restoration as a system, as a regulating law of social production... all progress in capitalistic agriculture is a progress in the art, not only of robbing the labourer, but of robbing the soil; all progress in increasing the fertility of the soil for a given time, is a progress towards ruining the lasting sources of that fertility.... Capitalist production, therefore, develops technology, and the combining together of various processes into a social whole, only by sapping the original sources of all wealth – the soil and the labourer.' (Marx 1967b, pp. 505-7)

In common with other writers, Foster lays great store by this passage (which is slightly different in the translation he uses) in showing the fertility of Marx's ideas as a resource for thinking about the relation between capitalism and ecological degradation (e.g. Foster, 2009; Foster et al, 2010) . He draws from it the importance of Marx's notion of an indispensable 'metabolism' through which human activity interacts with the rest of nature. In the case of capitalism, this metabolism is disturbed, as instanced by the interruption of the cycling of soil nutrients in the above example. Foster sees this 'metabolic rift' as a characteristic feature of capitalism, and generalises the idea as a way of explaining other aspects of our intensifying and multi-dimensional ecological crisis. Unlike many activists, for whom climate change is taken as the primary, or even sole, signifier of crisis, Foster draws on a wide range of scientific literature to expose the interacting diversity of dangerous environmental processes that we face. Rockström and others identify nine 'planetary boundaries' which together define the ecological space within which humans can live safely. So far as measures can be devised, each of these boundaries is being approached or actually breached by current industrial/economic expansion. Three ecological processes of degradation that have already transcended the boundaries are climate change, the disruption of the nitrogen cycle and biodiversity loss.

In the current phase of capitalist globalisation these several destructive (and self-destructive) processes amount to a global 'ecological rift', and mark the emergence of a new – and probably extremely short-lived – geological epoch, the 'anthropocene' (or 'capitalocene' as it is renamed by one of Foster's errant former students (Moore 2015)). Foster's broad framework for explaining the link between these destructive trends and the nature of capitalism is the domination of the logic of capital accumulation over that of the (qualitative, concrete) processes of producing use values, exacerbated by deregulated globalisation:

> 'Capital's insatiable appetite for ever-higher levels of profit and accumulation is reinforced by the domination of exchange value over use value, competition, and the concentration and centralization of capital. The impulse of incessant accumulation amplifies the social metabolism of society, increasing the demands placed on nature. New technologies are used above all to expand production and to lower labour costs. Capital's social metabolism is increasingly in contradiction with the natural metabolism, producing various metabolic rifts and forms of ecological degradation that threaten to undermine ecosystems.' (Foster et al 2010, pp. 406)

O'Connor, Polanyi and the 'second contradiction'

The work of Foster and others working with these ideas derived from Marx has been very influential and has inspired a growing body of substantial research, but it is not the only available route from Marx to socioecological analysis. Another very important contribution has been made by the late James O'Connor in the form of his identification of a 'second contradiction' of capitalism (see O'Connor 1996; see also the discussion of this idea, including eco-feminist arguments, in Benton (ed.) 1996). Though firmly within the historical materialist tradition, O'Connor argued that the full potential of that tradition for ecological understanding stands in need of some reworking and further development. Partly this has to do with the way the global ecological crisis of capitalism has emerged and taken its place as an urgent challenge to the future of humans in the period since Marx was writing, and, connectedly, that it was a dimension of his critique of capitalism that was little-developed compared with his attention to the dynamics of class antagonisms in the course of capitalist development. Although Foster is clearly right to draw attention to Marx's analysis of the metabolic rift in agriculture, it is worth noting that he (Marx) devoted only a few sentences on this in a short chapter mainly dealing with the dispersion of the agricultural labour force as a result of the growth of industry.

O'Connor's analysis is close to that of Karl Polanyi, in his major work

The Great Transformation (2001). Polanyi's work posed a challenge to the market fundamentalism of Hayek and others. The project of extending the sphere of commodity exchange ('the self-regulating market') to embrace the whole of social and economic life, he argued, is 'utopian', in the sense of 'no place', that is, impossible. For him, land, labour and money are fictitious commodities, in that they may be assigned a monetary value and bought and sold on the market, but do not behave as commodities. We might think of this in relation to labour. Labour (for Marx, labour-power) is bought and sold on what is called a labour market, equal pay for 'work of equal value' is demanded by women activists, and workers are warned not to 'price themselves out of a job'. But it is an odd sort of commodity that can be conscious of its own value, enter into combinations with other commodities and struggle to enhance its own value. But the sense in which labour (power) is a fictitious commodity goes deeper than this. While labour power is treated as if it were a commodity, its production and reproduction takes place outside the sphere of the market in various domestic arrangements in which human activities of many kinds, in forms of social relationship of many kinds, combine to restore the ability of workers to work day-by-day and reproduce them generation-by-generation to fill places in the economy as well as other non-economic institutions. In families and households the work involved is not in general directly paid, has purposes and an emotional and normative character quite other than that involved in the wage-relation, is not subject to the 'law of demand and supply' and so on. This is one important source for feminist gendered analysis and resistance (for example Dankelman & Davidson 1988; Soper 1995; Plumwood 1993; Mellor 1997).

Land as a fictitious commodity is subject to similar considerations. It is not produced at all, but given by nature, and insofar as it is worked on and transformed by socially combined humans to meet subsistence needs, this work has historically been that of communal or peasant associations, and always in recognition of the complex climatic, hydrological, geological and biological conditions which enable, limit and shape forestry, farming or horticulture in specific places.

Polanyi's argument is that in important respects the fictitious commodities are of necessity partly external to the system of commodity production and exchange, but at the same time make an indispensable contribution to it. Since key aspects of the production and reproduction of 'land' (nature?) and labour are provided free of charge (by domestic labour in the household, by human biological reproduction, by soil and ecosystems, etc.) the dynamic of cost-cutting and value expansion leads to downward pressure on these external practices, and their over-exploitation and degradation: impoverishment of families, loss of soil fertility, abandonment of agriculture for urban occupations and so on. However, as we saw in the above quotation from Marx, the soil and the labourer are the 'original sources of all wealth'. In degrading the processes that yield the 'fictitious commodities', the market is undermining its own conditions of existence. In Polanyi's version of the argument, the project of extending the sphere of the market to incorporate these external domains necessarily encounters limits and provokes resistances – what he called a 'countermovement' to the project of extending the commodification of nature and social processes. This might take (and historically has taken) many political forms, which generally, however, involve political constraints, or attempts to 're-embed' the market in society.

O'Connor's concept of a 'second contradiction' of capitalism drew on these arguments and those of Marx. If Marx had given central focus to the contradiction between forces of production and relations of production as the basis for the antagonism of labour and capital, relatively undeveloped in his thought was recognition of a second contradiction, between the forces and relations taken together, and their underlying conditions. In its bearing down on, degrading and destroying social cohesion, impoverishing families and households and over-exploiting natural systems, capital accumulation undermines its own conditions. In short, capitalism as an economic system is inherently unsustainable, both ecologically and socially.

So far, there are close parallels between Foster and his associates (advocates of the ecological Marx) and writers such as O'Connor, who offer some re-working of Marx's thought. An illustration of the difference is given by alternative understandings of Marx's account of the labour process. An extended passage at the beginning of part III of Volume 1 of *Capital* introduces the concept of the labour process. He distinguishes three factors (in abstraction from the social relations): the work itself, the subject of the work, and its instruments. In the labour-process, Marx says, [the worker]

> 'not only effects a change of form in the material on which he works, but he also realises a purpose of his own that gives the law to his *modus operandi*'.

So, the labour-process, as human activity, transforms its 'subject' according to a conscious purpose. It is a form of means/ends activity, but one which can, but does not always, engage the worker's mental and bodily powers, and be a source of enjoyment.

The second 'element' is the subject of labour. The subjects of labour are assigned to two categories.

First are those things that are acquired by simply severing their connexion with their environment: fruit, fish, wood from virgin forest, water, mineral ores and so on. These are the spontaneous provisions of nature. The other category of subjects of labour are materials (etc.) that have passed through, and been altered by, some previous labour process – these he terms, somewhat counter intuitively, 'raw materials'. The third element in the labour-process is the 'instrument of labour':

> 'An instrument of labour is a thing, or complex of things, which the labourer interposes between himself and the subject

of labour, and which serves as the conductor of his activity. He makes use of the mechanical, physical and chemical properties of some substances in order to make other substances subservient to his aims... Thus Nature becomes one of the organs of his activity, one that he annexes to his own bodily organs, adding stature to himself in spite of the bible... The earth itself is an instrument of labour, but when used as such in agriculture implies a whole series of other instruments and a comparatively high development of labour'. (Marx 1967b, pp. 178-9)

In these passages Marx represents the labour process as an instrumental activity, in which raw materials (or spontaneous provisions of nature) are altered by the use of bodily powers and/or instruments of various kinds, to yield a product that achieves a purpose conceptualised from the outset. To say that nature becomes an organ of human activity, or that the earth itself is an instrument of labour, is to suggest a Promethean view of production, such that the earth itself may become wholly subordinated to human purposes. Interestingly, as we saw above, this seems consistent with one possible interpretation of Marx's early account of the future communist society as realisation of the project of 'humanisation of nature'. In my own earlier commentaries on this issue (for example, Benton 1989; 2000) I tried to guard against this view of the labour process by distinguishing different 'intentional structures'; that is, depending on the kind of labour process, human intentions (the purposes of the worker, industry, etc.) are differently embedded in or articulated with the properties and powers of the various materials, forms of energy, processes etc. that are worked with or upon and conditions under which the work is conducted. In various ways these intentional structures enable but also set limits on what purposes can be achieved, and determine what intended or unintended consequences flow from the activity.

In the simplest classification, we can distinguish primary appropriation, ecoregulation and handicraft production. Primary appropriation corresponds to the activity of detaching and relocating for further use, some 'spontaneous provision of nature'. These labour processes by definition do not transform the subject of labour but simply appropriate it by detaching it from its naturally given context. But nature does not spontaneously produce things the humans need everywhere and at all times, and the activity of appropriating them can be more or less demanding. Marx mentions such subjects as fruit, fish, wood and mineral ores. In each case, activity is severely constrained in space by their geographical, hydrological, geological, climatic and/or ecological conditions and distributions. Fruit, fish, game and other gifts of nature are also available only within seasonal time-frames, and are often very demanding in terms of the knowledge and skills needed to 'detach' them from their context. Some 'spontaneous provisions' are absolutely limited in supply, while others have relative limits imposed by their own organic rates of reproduction and fecundity. As capitalist development progressively exhausts many of the natural resources on which it depends, costs of appropriating them rise and extractive industries become ever-more intensive and risky. As I write, exploratory 'fracking' for gas in the UK has yielded two earth-tremors in its first two days of operation.

If primary appropriation is an activity that is so severely constrained by its naturally given spatial, temporal, ecological, geographical, cognitive etc. conditions, ecoregulatory activity seems even less amenable to the simple model of production as conscious activity in which some instrument is used to transform a raw material (or spontaneous provision of nature) into a form that meets a human purpose. Forestry, agriculture, horticulture, conservation management and so on fall into this category of 'ecoregulation'. These activities resemble primary appropriation in that they are highly dependent on contextual conditions – altitude, aspect, climate, soil physics, chemistry and biology, plant and animal developmental rhythms, physiological requirements, reproductive systems and so on. Further, assuming these activities take place on land already cleared and prepared, with crop plants and domesticated animals already modified by previous processes of selection, hybridisation, etc., then the subsequent labour process consists primarily in optimising the conditions for autonomous processes of growth, development and flourishing in the crops or animals being farmed. So here, the transformative moment in the process is not brought about by the labour process itself, but is the outcome of autonomous organic processes taking place in the 'subject' of labour. Second, once agriculture (etc.) has become established, the primary purpose of agricultural labour is maintaining, regulating and reproducing the physical, chemical, hydrological, ecological etc. conditions under which domesticated organisms can grow, develop and reproduce in a way that yields use values that can be 'harvested' (secondary appropriation). In these processes, naturally given or socio-historically provided conditions (soil fertility, water, pest species, pollinators, and so on) figure both as 'subjects' of the labour process (i.e. they are the beings to which labour is applied) and also as conditions for it. This further disturbs the simple tripartite model of labour as transformative action.

Craft production seems closer to the means/ends intentional structure than either of the above, in that it works with energy and materials which generally have already been appropriated from nature, and often further transformed to become 'raw materials' in Marx's sense. Spatially and temporally, craft labour is thus much less constrained, and can, for example, be conducted indoors in a studio or workshop where internal conditions can be stabilised, tools and 'ancillary materials' provided and so on. Even here, though, it is important to recognise that those conditions are minimally required, as are the skills, strength and imagination of the craftsperson. But even if we focus narrowly on the relation between the worker and his/her 'subject', the activity is not wholly subordinated to its purpose, giving its 'law to his *modus operandi*' as Marx says. In fact, the interaction between agent and subject of labour is a reciprocal one in which the materiality of the subject offers resistances as well as opportunities, which may require revision of the *modus operandi,* and even of over-arching purposes, which themselves may not be defined in advance of the activity. Grayson Perry conveys something of this, together with recognition of the emotional content of craftwork:

> 'Craftsmanship is often equated with precision but I think there is more to it. I feel it is more important to have a long and sympathetic hands-on relationship with materials. A relaxed, humble, ever-curious love of stuff is central to my idea of being an artist.' (Grayson Perry 2011, p. 169)

To this short list of diverse sorts of labour processes, we could add many more: educating, nurturing, caring, nursing, conserving, cooking, cleaning as well as various sorts of industrial processes, data manipulation, scientific research, artistic and creative activities, musical composition and performance and so on. These all have intentional structures such that human purposes are present in each but variously embedded within, articulated with, constrained, enabled or shaped by a great range of psychological, social, biological, physical, chemical and so on conditions and processes. Some of these will be open to intentional modification in the course of a given phase of the labour process, others may depend on the development of ancillary technical accomplishments, while others may be ultimately beyond human intentional manipulation (e.g. the global climate, the biosphere, the incidence of solar radiation). In none of these labour processes is agency 'sovereign' in the way that would justify a Promethean or technological optimist grand narrative of ever-growing human 'mastery of nature'. Of course, none of this would have been news to Marx. This is quite clear from many passages in *Capital* and elsewhere. Foster cites a passage immediately prior to the ones I have analysed above to show just that:

> 'Labour is... a process between man and nature, a process by which man... mediates, regulates and controls the metabolism between himself and Nature.' (Marx 1976, p. 283)

However, we have seen that there are passages that can readily be interpreted in ways that would represent Marx as committed to a view of the historical process as one of mastery of nature through progressive 'development of the forces of production', outgrowing relations of production as they come to 'fetter' that development (see, for example, Cohen 1978). These compete with passages that resist such an interpretation, ones that have helpfully been selected and emphasised by ecological Marxists such as Burkett and Foster. What James O'Connor and others (including myself) have attempted is to develop more fully the indications provided by these passages in Marx.

The point of illustrating the diversity of 'intentional structures' characteristic of different labour processes was to indicate the micro-structure of a wider general contradiction between the capitalist mode of production and its conditions. Each of those labour processes depends on conditions which are discounted by the dominant mode of economic calculation as they come cost-free, or, to the extent that they are commodified, are over-exploited because their (non-monetary) costs of reproduction are discounted.

I will return, now, to O'Connor's concept of a second contradiction of capitalism. The second contradiction is understood as the tendency of capitalist development to override its own boundary conditions by degrading the conditions for the reproduction of labour power, degrading the socially provided infrastructures on which production depends (road and rail infrastructures, communications, flood defences and so on), and also degrading the free provisions of nature – climate, ecosystems, natural biodiversity, water, soil quality and so on. This analysis is close to that of Polanyi, both approaches depending on making an analytical distinction between those elements that enter into the process of production (labour, subject of production, means of production) and things, processes, conditions that are necessary for production but do not enter into it. It is precisely this distinction, essential for our analysis of the relation between capitalism and ecological degradation, that Marx 'forgets' when he writes of the earth itself as an instrument of labour.

In common with Polanyi, O'Connor sees the appropriation of unpaid reproductive labour, and the degradation of infrastructures and nature associated with capital accumulation as processes that necessarily provoke resistance, a 'countermovement'. For O'Connor this is the underlying genesis of the environmental movement and other social movements, especially the women's movement, that protest the impoverishment, disease, social dislocations, discrimination, environmental degradation and other harms imposed on populations, both through employment in capitalist firms and through familial, residential and other dimensions of life outside employment narrowly conceived. In demanding reforms to repair and invest in infrastructure, to conserve nature and natural resources, to mitigate air, water and soil pollution and so on it could be argued that these movements tend to save capitalism from itself – from undermining the very conditions that the system depends upon. These conditions, of course, include a degree of social cohesion and political legitimacy. So, the analysis moves beyond the narrowly economic analysis of the genesis of ecological degradation through capitalist economic development, and includes also an explanatory theory of the emergence of social movements such as feminism and environmental movements alongside the labour movement. Further, there is an answer to one of the questions posed above. That is, if capitalism has an inherent tendency to undermine its own conditions of existence, how come it has lasted so long? In brief, the answer is that spontaneously generated social movements induce action on the part of the modern capitalist state in the shape of welfare policy, public education, health and safety, public health measures and a wide range of environmental protections. Paradoxically, though they are often resisted by the representatives of capital, these reforms serve to protect capitalist development from its own self-destructive tendencies.

Questions

But there are further questions posed by this very promising basis for a green socialist politics.

First, in a phase of deregulated capitalist globalisation, the capacity of the national state effect amelioration of the destructive force of capital is limited, and its will to do so blunted by sources of economic and political power which transcend it. International popular mobilisation reached a high point in the early 1990s and effected some important goals in the 1992 'Earth Summit', but since then the forces of international destruction have been reasserted, partly as a result of ideological retreat by influential environmental NGOs, and partly by the rise to power of Trump and the extreme right in the USA, and, as I write this, the election of a president of the far right in Brazil.

Second, there are no guarantees that environmental and other social movements will make common cause with the labour movement. Much depends on the available cultural resources in any country and any particular time, the openness of communications media to counter-hegemonic struggles, the ideological and political strength and unity of ruling classes and class fractions and their political representatives, as well as the intensity and seriousness of the manifestations of degradation. For instance, in the UK just now the immiseration of many families by the application of universal benefit, with consequent massive increases in homelessness and use of food banks, the imposition of 'fracking' against the opposition of local people and their representative organisations, increasing experience of extreme weather events in the face of government failure to respond to recent intensification of scientific concern about climate change. We have an ecological Marxist analytical framework that links all these events and processes, but to translate that into forms of popular understanding in ways that connect diverse issues and grievances into a coherent popular political movement for transformation is an immense challenge. Nevertheless, it is one that can be met, and must be met if life on earth – especially human life – is to have a long-term future.

REFERENCES

T. Benton, *Philosophical Foundations of the Three Sociologies* (London & New York: Routledge, 1977, 2015).

T. Benton, "Marxism and natural limits: an ecological critique and reconstruction", *New Left Review* 178:51-86 (November-December 1989), reprinted in Benton (ed.) 1997.

T. Benton (ed.), *The Greening of Marxism.* (New York & London: Guilford, 1997).

T. Benton, "An ecological historical materialism", F. P. Gale & R. M. M'Gonigle (eds) *Nature, Production, Power* (Cheltenham, UK & Northampton Ma. USA: Edward Elgar, 2000).

P. Burkett, *Marx and Nature: a red and green Perspectives* (New York: St. Martin's, 1999).

G. A. Cohen *Karl Marx's Theory of History: a defence* (Oxford: Oxford University, 1978).

I. Dankelman & J. Davidson, *Women and Environment in the Third World* (London: Earthscan, 1998).

F. Engels *The Condition of the Working Class in England* (London: Panther, 1969).

J. B. Foster, *Marx's Ecology* (New York: Monthly Review, 2000).

J. B. Foster, B. Clark and R. York, *The Ecological Rift: Capitalism's War on the Earth* (New York: Monthly Review, 2010).

K. Marx & F. Engels, *The Communist Manifesto* (Harmondsworth: Penguin, 1967).

K. Marx, *Economic and Philosophic Manuscripts of 1844* (Moscow: Progress, 1967a).

K. Marx, *Capital Vol. I* (New York: International, 1967b).

K. Marx, *A Contribution to the Critique of Political Economy* (London: Lawrence & Wishart, 1971).

K. Marx, *Capital Vol. I* (New York: Vintage, 1971).

M. Mellor, *Feminism and Ecology* (New York: New York University, 1997).

J. W. Moore, *Capitalism in the Web of Life* (London & New York, 2015).

J. O'Connor, *Natural Causes: essays in ecological Marxism* (London & New York: Guilford, 1998).

G. Perry, *The Tomb of the Unknown Craftsman* (London: British Museum, 2011).

V. Plumwood, *Feminism and the Mastery of Nature* (London: Routledge, 1993).

K. Polanyi, *The Great Transformation* (Boston, Ma. USA: Beacon, 2001).

K. Soper, *What is Nature?* (Oxford, UK & Cambridge, Ma., USA, 1995).

15

From Socialist Calculation to Political Ecology

John O'Neill

Ted Benton in his chapter in this book provides an excellent account of environmental themes in Marx's own work and the subsequent discussion of these.

This chapter will not directly engage with Marx's own writings in any detail. Rather, it will be concerned with the implications of Marx's work for ongoing debates about the increasing monetisation, marketisation and financialisation of nature. The relation of Marx's work to these debates is mediated by another line of argument whose centenary anniversary we will soon be observing – the socialist calculation debates. A central legacy of Marx's work, which remains an area of dispute, concerns the nature and possibility of rational economic choices in a society beyond capitalism and commodity production. In an influential paper of 1920, Mises denied that rational economic choices were possible in a socialist society.[1] He was not the first to make that claim, but the paper was influential in opening the more widely known debates about socialist planning that followed. What has often been missed in the subsequent accounts of the debates was their important environmental dimensions, which were central to the development of later ecological economics. In this article I show why those often neglected dimensions of the debates retain their importance for current resistance to the increasing use of market modes of environmental governance. The first section of the chapter outlines the different dimensions of market modes of environmental governance and their problems. The second section traces the source of some of the central criticisms of these modes of governance in the socialist calculation debates.

I

Market modes of environmental governance have been increasingly prevalent in response to environmental problems. The natural world is conceived of as 'natural capital': habitats, sites of biodiversity, natural and cultural landscapes and a variety of other environmental goods are understood assets that provide 'benefit streams' – 'ecosystem services' – for human beings. As assets that provide benefit streams, they are open to substitution. The loss of one environmental asset, such as a woodland, wetland or an urban nature reserve, can be compensated for by the creation or enhancement of another environmental asset that provides the same services. As such, development that is destructive of one particular environmental good can take place as long as it is compensated for by a gain elsewhere, so that there is 'no net loss' or even 'net gain' to the ecosystem services.

The standard neo-classical account of the reason for the loss of environmental assets is that the assets are unpriced in markets (Arrow 1984, pp. 155). Preferences for environmental goods are not reflected in market prices. The solution is to ensure that they are priced. There are two main ways in which prices can be extended to environmental goods. First, public authorities can use decision-making procedures that mimic ideal markets by putting shadow prices on the goods which can then be entered into a cost-benefit analysis. These prices can be ascertained either by 'revealed preference' methods which infer a price from market behaviour – for example from differential house prices – or by 'stated preference' methods – asking people how much they would pay for the good if there were a market. Environmental goods and bads are thereby monetised. Second, the goods can be more directly marketised. Prices can be put onto environmental goods through the construction of actual markets in those goods, for example, through the introduction of tradeable rights to pollute and through the creation of tradeable assets in offsets. Emissions trading and offset markets are notable examples. With emissions trading, polluters are given rights to emit pollutants – such as CO_2 – within a total cap. These rights can be traded, the claim being that this produces the most efficient outcome by allowing pollution to be cut where it is cheapest to do so. Offset markets allow an environmentally damaging activity to be compensated by paying for a good or activity that offsets the effects of the damage. The emission of greenhouses gases can be offset by financing projects in areas such as forest and peatland protection, or the replacement of polluting factories in developing countries. Biodiversity offset markets work by giving environmental organisations or landowner credits for enhancing or protecting a site of biodiversity. Developers can buy these credits to offset the losses in biodiversity that they cause. Thus, there is no net loss of biodiversity.

The development of these markets in environmental goods and bads can, in turn, make possible a further independent development: the financialisation of nature. The new market mechanisms allow the goods to become valued not simply as benefit streams but as financial income streams. Like any other good that provides a financial income stream – from student loans to mortgage repayments – carbon-offset markets, biodiversity offset markets and emissions trading offer an asset class that has an associated financial income stream (Sayer 2015, p. 199; O'Neill 2017). As such it can be bundled with other income streams to create a financial asset with a particular level of risk and rate of return. The use of financial instruments, such as derivatives, can and are used to manage such risks.

There are a number of critical observations that can be made of the world of monetised, marketised and financialised nature that has developed as the dominant form of environmental governance. The assumption that environmental problems are primarily a matter of environmental preference not being reflected in market transactions fails to address the underlying structural causes of environmental damage. In particular it is blind to the systemic growth imperatives of capitalist society (Marx 1970, ch. 4). The financialised world of debt exacerbates this growth imperative: the very possibility of systematic repayment of debt with interest requires economic growth (Hayward, forthcoming, ch. 4). There are also more specific problems with offset markets (O'Neill 2017; Sullivan 2013), namely that offsets create a perverse asset class. The economic value of an environmental good as an offset depends upon the continuing existence of environmentally damaging activities. Without excessive carbon emission, a forest as a carbon offset is economically worthless. Without the loss of a site of biodiversity, a habitat as a biodiversity offset has no economic value. The result is a perverse structural dependence of nature conservation on environmentally damaging projects. Environmental organisations such as Conservation International, Flora and Fauna International, Kew Gardens, BirdLife International and the International Union for Conservation of Nature become financial beneficiaries of the 'no net loss' transfers from companies engaged in environmental damage.[2] Environmentalists appear as consultants to a new runway on the promise of money to offset emissions through peatland protection (Heathrow Airport Limited 2018; Webster 2017). Such dependencies are not a result of individual failings, but are a structural feature of offset markets (O'Neill 2017).

In addition to these arguments, there are arguments against the very possibility of using monetary exchange values to capture the value of environmental goods. One of the clearest skeptical statements about this possibility is that of K. William Kapp, one of the founders of modern ecological economics:

> 'The formulation of environmental policies, the evaluation of environmental goals and the establishment of priorities require a substantive economic calculus in terms of social use values (politically evaluated) for which the formal calculus in mon-

etary exchange values fails to provide a real measure – not only in socialist societies but also in capitalist economies. Hence the 'revolutionary' aspect of the environmental issue both as a theoretical and a practical problem. In short, we suggest that environmental values are social use values for which markets provide neither a direct measure nor an adequate indirect indicator.' (Kapp 1974, p. 38)

The reference to 'social use values' points back to the origins of this perspective in the work of Marx and Engels. Kapp's starting point is the environmental chapters in the socialist calculation debates that have been neglected, but now have renewed importance in the current context of market modes of environmental governance. The starting point to those debates is the claim that, as Marx put it in the *Grundrisse*, the end of capitalist society is the '[d]issolution of the mode of production and form of society based on exchange value'. (Marx 1973, p. 264). The distribution of labour and productive resources within capitalism is determined through exchange values in the market. Given that every society must distribute labour and productive resources, this raises the question of the form this must take in a socialist society in which their distribution no longer takes place through exchange-values. Marx and Engels both addressed the question primarily in terms of the distribution of social labour (Marx 1868; 1970 ch. 1 section 4; Engels 1878, p. 294-5). The question about whether decisions and priorities can be made in a mode of production that is not based on exchange value, and how, lies at the centre of the socialist calculation debates. For Kapp, the trajectory of those debates from that starting point into neo-classical models of market socialism involved a loss of insights central to the original debates that have come back to the fore with ecological problems. It is when one considers environmental decision-making that the limits of monetary exchange values come into sharp focus.

II

There is a standard story that is told of the socialist calculation debates. The story runs as follows.

In his 1920 paper Mises argued that rational economic choices would not be possible in a socialist society since socialist society would lack market prices in higher order production goods. In a complex modern economy, with its 'bewildering mass of intermediate products and potentialities of production' (Mises 1920; 1935, p. 103), there must be a single measure on the basis of which the relative value of different uses of productive resources in comparison with alternative uses could be calculated. In market economies, the exchange value of productive resources provides that common unit of measurement for comparing options: 'calculations based upon exchange values enable us to reduce values to a common unit' (Mises 1922; 1981

p. 99 cf. Mises 1920; 1935, p. 98). In the absence of private ownership of the means of production and hence a market in higher order production goods, there would exist no such market prices on the different factors of production. Rational calculation would be impossible. In the standard narrative, the central response to this argument is taken to be that of Lange (1936-7; 1964) and Taylor (1928; 1964). On their account, while a planning agency is not able to use actual market prices, it is able to mimic the ideal market of neo-classical theory through the use of shadow accounting prices. A socialist economy would have a market in consumer goods and free movement of labour, but lack a market in capital goods. However, using accounting prices, the central planning board, by a process of trial and error, would be able to mimic the textbook ideal neo-classical market to arrive at a set of equilibrium prices. On the standard narrative, the next chapter is provided by Hayek and epistemic arguments against central planning, which turn on the importance of dispersed knowledge local to time and space and practical knowledge, knowledge that cannot be passed onto a central planning board. This, in turn, generates responses. So goes the standard story, with different sides being assigned victory in the debate.

This standard narrative loses a number of dimensions of the debate and the protagonists in these debates have become increasingly relevant as market modes of environmental governance fail. One central dimension that is lost is the questioning of the presupposition on both sides of the standard debate that monetary values are both necessary and adequate for a rational economic choice. The standard debate revolves the Austrian scepticism about shadow accounting prices as an alternative to actual market prices and the neo-classical acceptance of the practice. That division has survived into more recent debates about shadow pricing.[3] The central question that Kapp raises – as to whether markets could provide either a direct or indirect measure of environmental values – is lost in this debate in the shift with the contributions of Lange and Taylor (Kapp 1974, pp. 36-37). Yet this was the central question in the earlier discussions – in particular with the contributions of Neurath and Weber (1974, p. 38). Hence, Kapp's earlier comment on the debates:

> 'the controversy initiated by O. Neurath, von Mises and Max Weber got sidetracked in various attempts to calculate the prices of productive factors by means of Walras' and Cassel's systems of equations and O. Lange's later elaboration of a theoretical model of "competitive socialism'. (Kapp 1955, p. 682)

Why does Kapp pick out the contributions of Neurath and Weber here? There are at least three dimensions of their contributions that matter to the question as to how far monetary measures are adequate for environmental governance: incommensurability of values, intergenerational impacts of economics decisions, and the nature of rational economic decision-making.

Otto Neurath's 1919 address to the Munich Worker's Council, 'The Character and Course of Socialization' (Neurath 1919; 1973), which he gave as the director of socialisation during the Bavarian revolution, was the occasion for Mises' 1920 paper on the impossibility of rational choice in a socialist economy. Neurath's address had defended plans for total socialisation that would form an 'economy in kind' – and economy *in natura* – in which money-values would no longer form the basis for economic calculation:

> 'We must at last free ourselves from outmoded prejudices and regard a large-scale economy in kind as a fully valid form of economy which is the more important today in that any completely planned economy amounts to an economy in kind. To socialize therefore means to further an economy in kind. To hold on to the split and uncontrollable monetary order and at the same time to want to socialize is an inner contradiction.' (Neurath 1919; 1973, p. 145)

It was this radical plan for an economy *in natura* that Mises responded to in his 1920 contribution.

> 'It is an illusion to imagine that in a socialist state calculation *in natura* can take the place of monetary calculation. Calculation *in natura*, in an economy without exchange, can embrace consumption goods only; it completely fails when it comes to dealing with goods of a higher order. And as soon as one gives up the conception of a freely established monetary price for goods of a higher order, rational production becomes completely impossible.' (Mises 1922; 1981, p. 13)

Lange, in defending his own neo-classical model of socialism, similarly rejected Neurath's proposals, endorsing Kautsky's criticisms of these plans, along with criticism of Marx and Engels' own account of planning in a socialist economy (Lange 1936-7; 1964, p. 135; Kautsky 1925; 2012, pp. 255-261). The debate between Lange and Mises becomes one only about the nature of prices to be extended to all productive resources. Should they be prices determined by actual market transactions or could shadow accounting prices be employed to guide the use of productive resources? In narrowing the scope of the debate, important arguments, developed in the earlier stages of the debates about the limits of monetary valuation, are lost in the subsequent exchanges between Mises and Lange. These are the arguments about the incommensurability of values, about the intergenerational impacts of economics decisions and about the nature of rational economic decision-making. It is these arguments that have become important in later ecological economics, in part through the work of Kapp.

The first set of arguments concerns the incommensurability of different dimensions of well-being and the variety and non-substitutability of goods required for their realisation. Thus, as Neurath notes in a later contribution to the journal of the Frankfurt School, *Zeitschrift for Sozialforschung*, in 1937, welfare concepts, such as the standard of living, are multidimensional:

> 'The attempts to characterize the standard of living are like those which try to characterize the "state of health". Both are multidimensional structures.' (1937; 2004, p. 520)[4]

There is no single measure of value, monetary or non-monetary, that is able capture those different dimensions of well-being. At the same time, the goods required to meet the different dimensions of well-being are heterogeneous and not substitutable for each other. The central claim being made here is a general one that will hold for any multi-dimensional approach to well-being that recognises the existence of thresholds in each dimension of well-being, be this a needs-based approach or one that appeals to capabilities (O'Neill 2010). Any such approach will entail forms of non-substitutability. If an agent suffers a loss in one dimension of well-being that takes her below a certain minimal threshold, it will not necessarily be the case that a gain will be had in some other dimension of well-being that compensates for that loss and maintains the same aggregate level of well-being. A person suffering from severe malnutrition requires specific nutritional goods to meet that need. Goods in some other dimension of well-being – say of education or leisure – will not be substitutes. To make this point is not to deny considerable causal relations between losses in different dimensions of well-being. The existence of compound inequalities is witness to the ways in which deficiencies in one dimension of well-being can lead to losses in others. However, remedies to those compounded inequalities must ultimately address deficiencies in each dimension of well-being, with the goods required to meet needs within that dimension. This point has implications for how we think about resource decisions across generations. If different dimensions of human flourishing require different goods for their realisation, then choices across generations that aim to maintain or improve the well-being of those in the future require each generation to pass on a bundle of goods that is disaggregated across the different dimensions of well-being (O'Neill, 2010).

The early socialist calculation debate had an intergenerational dimension that was missed in the later debate between different market based approaches. Neurath's criticism of using any single unit of measurement of value over different plans was aimed not just at criticising the market and monetary measures, but also other suggested single units, be they labour time defended by some socialists or the energy units associated by the early precursors of an energy economics such as Popper-Lynkeus and Ballod-Atlanticus. All had problems in considering intergenerational uses of resources. Market-based approaches fail since the needs and wants of future generations cannot be expressed in behaviour in current markets. Labour time measures fail to address the effects of the use of energy and resources in current labour time saving for future generations. However, energy units fail to consider the effects of energy saving on the quality of labour in current conditions:

'The question might arise, should one protect coal mines or put greater strain on men? The answer depends for example on whether one thinks that hydraulic power may be sufficiently developed or that solar heat might come to be better used, etc. If one believes the latter, one may 'spend' coal more freely and will hardly waste human effort where coal can be used. If however one is afraid that when one generation uses too much coal thousands will freeze to death in the future, one might use more human power and save coal. Such and many other non-technical matters determine the choice of a technically calculable plan... we can see no possibility of reducing the production plan to some kind of unit and then to compare the various plans in terms of such units...' (Neurath 1928; 1973, p. 263)

Measures of inter-generational well-being and the resources required to meet them had to themselves be multi-dimensional.

The third set of arguments in the early socialist calculation debate that got lost in later versions concerns the nature of rational economic decision-making as such. Kapp's reference to the importance of Weber's contribution is concerned with this aspect of the debate.[5] The importance of Weber's contribution, in contrast to that of Mises, is that Weber is much more careful than Mises in distinguishing the different senses in which economic decisions can be described as rational. Specifically, in responding to Neurath's socialisation plans (Weber 1921-22; 1978, ch. 2, sections 12-14), he draws a distinction between formal and substantive rationality:

'The term 'formal rationality of economic action' is used to designate the extent of quantitative calculation or accounting which is technically possible and which is actually applied. The 'substantive rationality', on the other hand, is the degree to which the provisioning of a given group of persons (no matter how delimited) with goods is shaped by economically orientated social action under some criterion ... of ultimate values, regardless of the nature of these ends'. (Weber 1921-22; 1978, p. 85)

Weber does take formal rationality to be best realised through monetary calculations based on exchange values:

From a purely technical point of view, money is the most "perfect" means of economic calculation. That is, it is formally the most rational means of orienting economic activity. Calculation in terms of money, and not its actual use, is thus the specific means of *instrumentally* rational economic provision. (Weber 1921-22; 1978, p. 86)

Hence, he argues that Neurath's socialist economy in kind would be less formally rational than a capitalist economy. However, unlike Mises, Weber does not identify formal rationality with rationality as such. Economies could still be open to judgement in terms of their substantive rationality according to some ends where '"purely formal" rationality of calculation in monetary terms is of quite secondary importance or even is fundamentally inimical to their respective ultimate ends...' (Weber 1921-22; 1978, p. 86). The reason Weber's contribution is so important for early ecological economists like Kapp lies in his recognition of the importance of substantive rationality. Monetary measures might improve calculability in economic choices. They do not thereby make them more rational in the substantive sense. Thinking about environmental goods requires the exercise of substantive rationality. Hence, Kapp's claim quoted above:

The formulation of environmental policies, the evaluation of environmental goals and the establishment of priorities require a substantive economic calculus in terms of social use values (politically evaluated) for which the formal calculus in monetary exchange values fails to provide a real measure – not only in socialist societies but also in capitalist economies. (Kapp 1974, p. 38)

The distinctions are redeployed by Kapp and Polanyi in developing central themes in the criticism of standard approaches to economics generally and to the limits of markets with respect to environmental goods in particular.

Kapp retains the original Weberian distinction between formal and substantive rationality. Formal rationality refers to accounting in numerical terms as exemplified in capital accounting. Substantive rationality is concerned with the economy insofar as it is concerned with meeting human needs by the physical and social resources available. It requires democratic deliberation about our needs, not simply calculation. And insofar as it requires calculation, it requires 'calculation in real terms rather than in terms of prices' (Kapp 1963, p. 195):

As far as social benefits are concerned the criteria available are social minima based upon a substantive and democratic evaluation of social needs and requirements and their comparison in real (physical) terms. (Kapp 1963, p. 195)[7]

The appeal here is to 'quantitative input-output analysis', work taken up subsequently in ecological economics in the analysis of the material and energy flows through the economy.

Polanyi, while he starts from Weber in making his distinction between formal and substantive economics, reworks the concept of formal rationality.[8] It is transformed from its Weberian sense of rationality concerned with calculability and is taken to refer to economic rationality in the sense that Robbins introduces the concept, as a process of choice between different ends in conditions in which the means are not sufficient to realise them all, but rather have alternative uses. Substantive economics, in contrast, is concerned with the provisioning of goods to meet human needs and wants. Formal economic rationality is tied to the market economy. Outside of the market economy it loses its relevance. One is concerned rather with the substantive economy, the economy understood as 'an instituted process of interaction between man and his environment, which results in a continuous supply of want-satisfying material means' (Polanyi 1957, p. 248). The argument again is that it is an error to use the forms of formal rationality found within market economics to define the nature of rational economic behaviour:

> 'the substantive definition of "economic"... permits a redefinition of the main economic institutions that does not take as its frame of reference the market.' (Polanyi 1950, p. 61, emphasis in the original)

What both Kapp and Polanyi retain from the earlier debates is a recognition of the rational limits of monetary valuation, in particular when it comes to environmental goods. Modern neo-classical economics start from the assumption that rational choice requires pricing. Its Austrian critics share the same assumption, but reject the claim that shadow prices are an alternative to actual prices in the market place, hence their appeal for free market solutions to environmental problems. What the failure of, and resistance to, those market-based approaches reveal is the deep problems with both perspectives. The response to the failure of market modes of governance can take a variety of forms. Some, like Kapp, call for social and democratic modes of decision-making using not monetary measures but direct physical, environmental and social measures of both welfare and resources. More radical versions of this view ultimately aim, as did Neurath, at a generalised decommodification of goods, replacing markets with non-market economic institutions (Neurath 1920; O'Neill 2011). Other responses, such as that of Polanyi, are critical not of markets as such[9], but of the disembedding of markets from the constraints of social and environmental norms in market societies through the creation of the fictitious commodities in labour, land and money (Polanyi 1957; Dale 2010, ch. 5).

What these views and the later forms of ecological economics influenced by them share, as an inheritance from the early socialist calculation debates, is the view that monetary values cannot capture the ways in which environmental goods matter to human well-being.[10] There is no single monetary measure of well-being. There is no single measure of the value of resources that meets human needs. The attempt to treat social relationships and relationships to nature simply as forms of social and natural capital fails to understand their role in flourishing human lives. Relationships to particular people and places that are constitutive of well-being block their substitutability (O'Neill 2017). Marketisation compounds those problems. Losses of goods central to human well-being cannot be offset by gains elsewhere that compensate for those losses. Financialisation distances economic decisions still further from the real material and social conditions for the goods of human life. The limits of market valuation and market modes of governance become still clearer in the context of environmental limits to economic activity. Such limits can only be specified in terms of real physical and bio-physical indicators. How we are to respond to them requires a specification of the physical and bio-physical throughput of the economy and the rich set of needs that this must satisfy and plans to meet these. In the context of climate change the need for a shift from market modes of governance has never been more pressing. What I have tried to show here is both the influence of the early contributions to the socialist calculation debates to the development of these ecological criticisms of market governance and of their continuing relevance.

NOTES

1 See Mises 1920 and 1922.

2 For example, Rio Tinto has entered into partnerships with Conservation International, Flora and Fauna International, Kew Gardens, BirdLife International and the International Union for Conservation of Nature in Madagascar (Seagle 2012, p. 453). For details of the partnership between Rio Tinto and BirdLife International and its role in the development of Rio Tinto's offsetting pilot project in Madagascar see BirdLife International 2011. On the impacts on the local community see Kill, J. and Franchi G. 2016 and Seagle 2012.

3 Mark Sagoff in particular has combined criticism of the practice of shadow pricing environmental goods for the purposes of cost-benefit analysis with an endorsement of an Austrian approach to markets and the environment. See Sagoff 2008, pp. 80-81 and passim. For a discussion see O'Neill 2012.

4 The same edition contained Horkheimer's influential criticism of the left Vienna Circle of which Neurath was a leading member, 'The Latest Attack on Metaphysics' (Horkheimer 1937; 1974). The subsequent fall out led to a bifurcation of political ecology between the physicalist and materialist tradition represented by Neurath and the criticisms of science, scientism and instrumental reason that developed within the Frankfurt School. For a discussion and suggestion for a partial reconciliation, see O'Neill and Uebel 2018.

5 For a discussion see Uebel 2018.

6 In the English translation by Talcott Parsons the word 'instrumental' is absent undermining the actual meaning of the statement. In the original German version Weber speaks explicitly of "Zweckrationalität" (instrumental rationality) (1921-22; 1972, p. 45). My thanks to Christian Scholz for pointing this out.

7 Kapp refers specifically back to Neurath's work and Weber's critical commentary on it in developing this point (Kapp 1963, p. 196).

8 The important influence in this transformation is the second edition of Menger's *Grundsätze der Volkswirtschaftslehre*. For a discussion see Dale 2010, pp. 103-114. See also Berger 2008 on the correspondence between Kapp and Polanyi on substantive economics.

9 Polanyi's own early contribution to the socialist calculation debate had rejected Neurath's marketless socialism (Polanyi 1922; 2016, p. 398) and defended a form of 'functionally organised socialist economy' influenced by Cole's guild socialism. For a discussion see Dale 2016, ch.3.

10 See Martinez-Alier 1990.

BIBLIOGRAPHY

Arrow, K. 1984, 'Limited Knowledge and Economic Analysis' in *The Economics of Information* Cambridge MA: Harvard University Press.

Berger S. 2008 Karl Polanyi's and Karl William Kapp's Substantive Economics: Important Insights from the Kapp–Polanyi Correspondence, *Review of Social Economy*, 66, pp. 381-396.

BirdLife International (2011) *Tsitongambarika Forest, Madagascar. Biological and Socio-economic Surveys, with Conservation Recommendations.* Cambridge, UK: BirdLife International.

Dale, G. 2010 *Karl Polanyi: The Limits of the Market* Cambridge: Polity Press.

Dale, G. 2016 *Karl Polanyi: A Life on the Left* New York: Columbia University Press.

Engels 1878 *Anti-Duhring* Marx K. and Engels F. *Collected Works, Volume 25,* London: Lawrence and Wishart, 1987.

Hayward, T. forthcoming *Global Justice and Finance* Oxford: Oxford University Press.

Heathrow Airport Limited 2018 *Heathrow 2.00: Carbon Neutral Growth Roadmap* https://www.heathrow.com/file_source/Company/Static/PDF/Communityandenvironment/Carbon-Neutral-Growth-Roadmap.pdf

Horkheimer, M. 1937 'Der neueste Angriff auf die Metaphysik', *Zeitschrift für Sozialforschung* 6 pp. 4-53, translated as 'The Latest Attack on Metaphysics' in Horkheimer, *Critical Theory. Selected Essays,* New York: Seabury Press, 1972, pp. 132-187.

Kapp, K.W. 1955 'Review: *Einführung in die Theorie der Zentralverwaltungswirtschaft* by K. Paul Hensel'. *American Economic Review* 45, pp. 682–5.

Kapp, K.W. 1963 'Social Costs and Social Benefits – Their Relevance for Public Policy and Economic Planning' in *Hindu Culture, Economic Development, and Economic Planning in India* Bombay: Asia Publishing House.

Kapp, K. W. 1974 *Environmental Policies and Development Planning in Contemporary China and Other Essays* Paris: Mouton.

Kautsky. K. 1925 *The Labour Revolution* London: Routledge, 2012.

Kill, J. and Franchi G. 2016 *Rio Tinto's biodiversity offset in Madagascar* World Rainforest Movement and Re-Common.

Lange, O. 1936-7 'On the Economic Theory of Socialism' in B. Lippincott ed. *On the Economic Theory of Socialism* New York: McGraw-Hill, 1964.

Martinez-Alier, *Ecological Economics*, Oxford:Blackwell, 1987, 2nd ed. 1990.

Marx, K. 1868 'Letter to Ludwig Kugelmann, 11 July 1868' Marx, K and Engels, F. *Collected Works, Volume 43* Lawrence and Wishart: London, 2010, pp. 67-70.

Marx, K. 1970 *Capital I* London: Lawrence and Wishart.

Marx, K. 1973 *Grundrisse* London: Penguin.

Mises, L. 1920 ‚Die Wirtschaftsrechnung im sozialistischen Gemeinwesen',

Archiv für Sozialwissenschaft 47, trans. 'Economic Calculation in the Socialist Commonwealth' in F.A. Hayek (ed.), *Collectivist Economic Planning*, London: Routledge and Sons, 1935, pp. 89-130.

Mises, L. 1922 *Die Gemeinwirtschaft*. Jena; Fischer, trans. *Socialism*, Indianapolis: Liberty Press, 1981.

Neurath, O. 1919 *Wesen und Weg der Sozialisierung*, Munich: Callwey, trans. 'Character and Course of Socialisation' in Neurath 1973, *Empiricism and Sociology* ed. by M. Neurath and R.S. Cohen, Dordrecht: Reidel, 1973, pp. 135-150.

Neurath O. 1928, *Lebensgestaltung und Klassenkampf*, Berlin: Laub, excerpts translated as 'Personal Life and Class Struggle', in *Empiricism and Sociology* (ed. by M. Neurath and R.S. Cohen), Dordrecht: Reidel, 1973, pp. 249-298.

Neurath, O. 1937 'Inventory of the Standard of Living', *Zeitschrift für Sozialforschung* 6, pp. 140-151, reprinted in Neurath, *Economic Writings. Selections 1904-1945* (ed. by T. Uebel and R.S.Cohen), Dordrecht: Kluwer, 2004, pp. 513-526.

O'Neill, J. 2010 'The Overshadowing of Need' in Felix Rauschmayer, Ines Omann, Johannes Frühmann eds. *Sustainable Development: Capabilities, Needs, and Well-Being* London: Routledge.

O'Neill, J. 2011 'Money, Markets and Ecology' in A. Nelson and F. Timmerman eds. *Life Without Money: Building Fair and Sustainable Economies* London: Pluto Press.

O'Neill, J. 2012 'Austrian Economics and the Limits of Markets' *Cambridge Journal of Economics* 36, pp. 1073–1090.

O'Neill, J. 2017 *Life Beyond Capital* Centre for the Understanding of Sustainable Prosperity, 2017 https://www.cusp.ac.uk/wp-content/uploads/Life-beyond-capital-online.pdf.

O'Neill, J. And Uebel, T. 2018 'Between Frankfurt and Vienna: Two Traditions of Political Ecology' K. Forrester and S. Smith eds. *Nature, Action and the Future*. Cambridge: Cambridge University Press.

Polanyi, K. 1922 'Sozialistische Rechnungslegung' *Archiv für Sozialwissenschaft und Sozialpolitik* 49, pp. 377–420, Bockman, J. and Fischer, A. and Woodruff, D. trans. 'Socialist accounting' *Theory and Society*, 45, 2016, pp. 398-427.

Polanyi, K. 1950 'The Contribution of Institutional Analysis to the Social Sciences' in K. Polanyi *For a New West: Essays, 1919-1958* Cambridge, Polity, 2014.

Polanyi, K. 1957 'The Economy as Instituted Process', in K. Polanyi, C. Arensberg and H. Pearson eds. *Trade and Market in the Early Empires* The Free Press, New York.

Sagoff M. 2008 *The Economy of the Earth* second edition Cambridge: Cambridge University Press.

Sayer, A. 2015 *Why We Can't Afford the Rich* Bristol: Policy Press.

Seagle, C. 2012, 'Inverting the impacts: Mining, conservation and sustainability claims near the Rio Tinto/QMM ilmenite mine in Southeast Madagascar', *The Journal of Peasant Studies*, 39, pp. 447-477.

Sullivan, S. 2013 'After the Green Rush? Biodiversity Offsets, Uranium Power and the Calculus of Casualties in Greening Growth' *Human Geography* 6, pp. 80-101.

Taylor, F. 1928 'The Guidance of Production in a Socialist State' in B. Lippincott ed. *On the Economic Theory of Socialism* New York: McGraw-Hill, 1964.

Uebel, T. 2018 'Calculation in Kind and Substantive Rationality: Neurath, Weber, Kapp' *History of Political Economy* 50, pp. 289-320.

Weber, M. 1921-2 *Wirtschaft und Gesellschaft. Grundriss der verstehenden Soziologie*, Tübingen: Mohr (Siebeck), 4th rev. ed. 1956, trans. *Economy and Society. An Outline of Interpretive Sociology*, Berkeley: University of California Press, 1978.

Webster, B. 2017 'Prince's Green Guru is Paid to Help Heathrow' *The Times* March 2,
www.thetimes.co.uk/article/prince-s-green-guru-is-paid-to-help-heathrow-d2zzc7ws8.

16

The Enduring Legacy of Karl Marx

Sitaram Yechury

At the outset, in a nutshell, I would like to outline how the Indian communists, the Communist Party of India (Marxist) in particular, have internalised Marxism.

Marxism is unique in the sense that it can be transcended only when its agenda is realised; the agenda of realising a classless communist social order. Specifically, under capitalism, its understanding of capitalism is alone thorough enough for it to comprehend the historical possibilities that lie beyond it. Hence Marxism can never be, under capitalism, rendered superfluous until capitalism is itself superseded.

Post-capitalism, Marxist philosophy and its world view will continue to be the basis and the scientific guide for socialist construction and the transition to communism.

Marxism is not a dogma but a 'creative science'. It is based on, among other things, 'a concrete analysis of concrete conditions'. Marxism is an approach to the analysis of history in general, and of capitalism in particular. It is on this basis, building on the foundation provided by Marx, that we continuously enrich our theory for understanding the present conjuncture and the possibilities it holds for the future. Far from being a closed theoretical system, Marxism represents a process of continuous theoretical enrichment.

It is precisely due to this – 'creative science' – that Marxism alone is capable of identifying the tendencies and direction of developments which are the consequences of the perennial human-nature dialectic, encompassing all areas of human endeavour.

Every single scientific discovery and development – from astro-physics to nano-technology – resoundingly validates dialectical materialism. Marxism alone is able to anticipate and equip us to deal with situations that arise when artificial intelligence threatens to take over and control our lives.

Today's world – imperialist globalisation

The post-Second World War decades of peaceful development of global capitalism, through the period of the Cold War, led to gigantic levels of capital accumulation. This was further augmented in the last decade of the 20th century following the collapse of the Soviet Union and the return of the former USSR and East European socialist countries into the orbit of capitalism. This gigantic accumulation led to the emergence and consolidation of international finance capital propelling accumulation and centralisation of capital to even higher levels.

The current phase of globalisation, within the stage of imperialism, is leading to further and higher levels of capital accumulation directed by international finance capital. This international finance capital is, today, enmeshed with industrial and other forms of capital in its pursuit of profit maximisation. International finance capital now leads the commonality of purpose to unleash fresh attacks to vastly increase the levels of capital accumulation and profit maximisation even further.

Such reordering of the world for profit maximisation under the dictates of international finance capital, defines neo-liberalism. It operates, firstly, through policies that remove restrictions on the movement of goods and capital across borders. Trade liberalisation displaces domestic producers engendering domestic deindustrialisation, particularly in developing countries. This also happens in the developed countries due to relocation of production and business operations outside their countries. So also, the liberalisation of capital flows allows multinational corporations to acquire domestic productive assets abroad (like India's public sector), vastly enlarging capital accumulation.

Other ways of consolidating capital accumulation are through the imposition of deflationary policies like restrictions on government expenditures in the name of fiscal discipline (making available larger quantum of liquidity to international finance capital to multiply speculative profits), which leads to the lowering of the level of aggregate demand in the world economy; a shift in the terms of trade against the peasantry in the developing countries; a rolling back of the state sector in providing social services globally, more pronounced in the developing countries, which increasingly become privatised and the opening up of huge new areas of public utilities for profit maximisation. Intellectual property rights and other forms of monopoly control over knowledge generates massive profits through the control over the production and reproduction of knowledge. Thus, a new feature of contemporary imperialism is the coercive prising open of new and hitherto non-existent avenues for profit maximisation.

All through the history of capitalism, accumulation takes place in two ways: one is through the normal dynamics of capital expansion (appropriation) – through the unfolding of its production process – and the other is through coercion and outright looting (forcible expropriation), a brutality Marx defines as the primitive accumulation of capital. Primitive accumulation is often erroneously interpreted as a historical category – primitive versus modern.

For Marx and therefore Marxists, primitive accumulation is an analytical category that historically continues to co-exist with the normal dynamics of capitalism. The process of primitive accumulation has taken various forms in the past, including direct colonisation. The aggressiveness of primitive accumulation, at any point of time, is directly dependent on the balance of international correlation of class forces which either permit or inhibit the manifestation of such capitalist brutality. In the current phase of contemporary imperialism, the intensification of such a process of brutal, primitive accumulation is assaulting a vast majority of of the world's population, both in the developing as well as the developed countries.

It is this predatory capitalist character for constant profit maximisation that is sharply widening the economic inequalities globally and domestically in every country, while, at the same time, imposing greater miseries on the vast majority of global working people and the poor. Every effort to emerge from one phase of the current systemic crisis is, naturally, leading to a newer phase of a deeper crisis because of the very nature of the laws of capitalist development.

Crisis of neo-liberalism – political rightward shift

Currently, nearly a decade after the global financial meltdown, neo-liberalism itself is in a crisis.

It has by now become clear to a large number of people, particularly in the developed capitalist countries, that the rise of neo-liberalism, which in a sense was preceded by the rise of Reagan and Thatcher in the US and UK, had created conditions whereby the bulk of the economic development and growth has been garnered by the miniscule minority leaving greater misery for the vast majority of the people. In the first two-and-a-half post-Second World War decades, global capitalism saw a dynamic period of growth often referred to as the Golden Age of Capitalism.

In the USA, in the period 1948 to 1972, every section of the American population experienced an increase in the standard of living. However, between 1972 and 2013, the bottom 10% experienced a fall in real incomes while the top 10% did excessively well. The median real income for full-time male workers is now lower than it was four decades ago. The income of the bottom 90% of the population has stagnated for over 30 years. On average, 65-70% of households in 25 high-income economies experienced stagnant or lower real incomes between 2005 and 2014. According to a Gallup poll in 2000, only 33% of Americans called themselves working class. By 2015, the figure was 48%, almost half the population. The misery of this vast section of the global population and such obscene levels of inequality has created discontent of huge proportions, which is seeking a political expression.

This crisis of neo-liberalism has created new contradictions leading to ruptures, conflicts among imperialist countries, such as Brexit. Emergence of new political forces and rising tensions are the order of the day.

The current period is witnessing a further political rightward shift in many parts of the world. In the face of the current crisis, imperialism pursues aggressive neo-liberalism combined with a global divisive agenda fostering domestic, local and regional tensions. It engages in military interventions to consolidate its global hegemony and control of economic resources, like oil in West Asia. This engenders the growth of racism, xenophobia and extreme right-wing neo-fascist tendencies. The triumph of Donald Trump in the US elections, the right-wing mobilisation in the Brexit vote in Britain, the electoral gains of Marine Le Pen of the extreme-right National Front in France, the advance of the Alternative for Deutschland in Germany, the formation of a right-wing government in Austria which includes the extreme-right Freedom Party, and representation of nearly a third of the European Parliament MPs from right-wing and extreme right-wing political parties are a reflection of this rightward shift. This tendency has also its consequent reflection in Indian politics.

In times of intense global economic crisis, a political battle surfaces over who will marshal the rising popular discontent. The political right-wing advances by rallying popular discontent and in ensuring that the Left and progressive forces do not emerge as a major political force. These right-wing forces capitalising on people's discontent end up pursuing precisely those very economic policies that have led to this economic crisis, imposed unprecedented burdens on the people and caused the rise in popular discontent in the first place.

Socialist alternative

It is clear that in the coming days, the political direction in many of the countries of the world will be determined by the political success in marshalling popular discontent between the left-oriented democratic forces and the political right. Fascism arose with the support of the world's monopoly capital in the wake of the Great Depression of 1929-30. Fascist forces were able to successfully exploit the growing popular discontent among the people as a consequence of the crisis. In the current conjuncture, the rising popular discontent against the prolonged economic crisis is fuelling the rise of extreme right and neo-fascist forces.

The socialist ideal remains, in today's conditions of global capitalist crisis, the only manner in which humanity can emancipate itself from exploitation. Since the 2008 global financial meltdown, global capitalism has plunged from one crisis into another. Every effort to overcome the crisis has laid the seeds of a deeper crisis. It has become increasingly clear – with the unprecedented economic burdens imposed through intensified capitalist exploitation on the people, consequent sharply widening economic inequalities and the immiseration of vast sections of global population – that the predatory nature of capitalism has assumed a more naked form.

No amount of reforms within capitalism can liberate humanity from the clutches of such exploitation. It is only the political alternative of socialism that can achieve this purpose. The assault on the rule of capital by this political alternative of socialism has to be intensified for eventual human liberation from exploitation.

Capitalism never collapses automatically whatever may be the intensity of the crisis. Unless a political alternative develops to challenge capitalism, capitalism invariably survives by intensifying human exploitation. Hence, the strength of the socialist political alternative has to grow vastly. While there are growing struggles all across the globe against the current predatory expression of capitalist plunder and the accompanying imperialist hegemonic aggression, these popular mobilisations continue to remain essentially defensive; defensive in the sense that people are in the midst of struggles to defend their existing democratic rights and livelihood conditions. It is such struggles that must accumulate to reach the levels of mounting the class assault against the rule of capital.

Capitalism, therefore, requires to be overthrown. This depends decisively on the strengthening of that material force in society led by the working-class which can mount, through popular struggles, the intensification of the class struggle to launch the political offensive against the rule of capital. The building of this material force and its strength is the 'subjective factor', the strengthening of which is the essential imperative. The objective factor – the concrete situation of the crisis – however conducive it may be for a revolutionary advance, cannot be transformed into a revolutionary assault against the rule of capital without the strengthening of this 'subjective factor'.

Various intermediary slogans, measures and tactics will have to be employed by the working class, based on a concrete analysis of concrete conditions in each country, to sharpen class struggles and to meet the challenges of these real conditions in order to strengthen the 'subjective factor' and, thus, advance the process of revolutionary transformation in their respective countries. The political correlation of forces amongst the people must shift in favour of the Left. This will happen only through the unleashing of militant popular struggles on the basis of an alternative policy framework against neo-liberalism. In the absence of this, it is the political right which consolidates popular discontent in its favour.

Marxism alone today provides the ideological foundations and the theoretical underpinning for strengthening the 'subjective factor' and, thus, sharpening class struggles. Marxism, therefore, remains and shall remain, as long as capitalism is not superseded, the only potent force for changing the real world today, for changing this world for the better, to end the exploitation of humans by humans and nations by nations.

AUTHOR BIOGRAPHIES

Ted Benton

Ted Benton is emeritus professor of Sociology at University of Essex. He was one of the founders of critical realist philosophy, and has written extensively on philosophy of social science, the thought of Louis Althusser, animal rights, biology and society, sociology of power, political economy of ecological crisis and other topics. His most recent work includes a biography of the pioneering evolutionist and socialist, Alfred Russel Wallace and numerous books on insect groups such as bees, butterflies, dragonflies and crickets. He is a founder member of the Red-Green Study Group, and of the recently formed Beyond Extinction Economics network (BEE).

Alan Blackwell

Alan Blackwell is Professor of Interdisciplinary Design at the University of Cambridge, and Research Director of the Cambridge Global Challenges initiative. He has worked as an Artificial Intelligence Engineer for Hitachi Ltd and Arthur D Little Cambridge Consultants, with extensive experience of automation engineering in the food processing and transport industries. His research extends from social critique of technology to commercial, artistic and humanitarian applications of academic research.

Mary Davis

Mary Davis is Visiting Professor of Labour History at Royal Holloway, University of London. She has written, broadcast and lectured widely on women's history, labour history, imperialism and racism. She was awarded the TUC Women's Gold Badge in 2010 for services to trade unionism. She is one of the founder members of the Sylvia Pankhurst Memorial Committee and 'A Charter for Women'.

Francisco Dominguez

Francisco Dominguez is a senior lecturer at Middlesex University, London, UK, where he is head of the Latin American Studies Research Group. He is also the National Secretary of the Venezuela Solidarity Campaign. Dr Dominguez arrived in Britain in 1979 as a Chilean political refugee. He is a specialist on Latin America's political economy, especially Venezuela and Cuba, about which he has written and published extensively. He is co-editor of *Right-Wing Politics in the New Latin America* (Zed, 2011) and co-author of *Right Politics in the New Latin America* (Zed, 2016).

Ben Fine

Ben Fine is Professor of Economics at the School of Oriental and African Studies, University of London. He is author of <u>Marx's *Capital*</u>, with Alfredo Saad Filho, now in its sixth edition, and has been winner of the Deutscher Prize and the Myrdal Prize for other books.

John Foster

John Foster is emeritus professor and a member of the editorial boards of *Social History* and *Theory & Struggle*. He is currently Secretary of the Marx Memorial Library Education Committee. His most recent publication is *The Councils of Action 1920* (2017).

Ursula Huws

Ursula Huws is Professor of Labour and Globalisation at the University of Hertfordshire in the UK. She has been carrying out pioneering research on the economic and social impacts of technological change, the restructuring of employment and the changing international division of labour for many years. She is the editor of the international interdisciplinary peer-reviewed journal *Work Organisation, Labour and Globalisation* and co-edits the Palgrave Macmillan/Springer Dynamics of Virtual Work book series.

Christine Lindey

After graduating from the Courtauld Institute, Christine Lindey taught art history in various London colleges including Birkbeck College University of London and the University of the Arts. She specialises in 19th and 20th century art with a particular interest in socialist and Soviet art. Her book *Art in the Cold War from Kalamazoo to Vladivostok* (1990), which is still in print, pioneered the comparative study of Soviet and Western art. Her latest book is *Art for All: British Socially Committed Art from the 1930s to the Cold War*. Christine's exhibition reviews appear in the *Morning Star*.

David Margolies

David Margolies is Emeritus Professor of English at Goldsmiths, University of London. He edited *Red Letters* for ten years and has published a great deal on Shakespeare. Recently he has published an anthology of Christopher Caudwell.

John McDonnell MP

John McDonnell is the Shadow Chancellor of the Exchequer. He has been the Labour Member of Parliament for Hayes and Harlington since the 1997 general election.

David McLellan

David McLellan is a Fellow of Goldsmith's College, University of London and Emeritus Professor of Political Theory, University of Kent. He is the author of numerous books on Marx and Marxism, principally *Karl Marx: A Biography*, which is now in its 4th edition.

Isabel Monal

Isabel Monal is an Academician Emeritus at the Cuban Academy of Sciences. Her texts have been translated into eight languages and published in more than 15 countries (in four continents). She received the Social Sciences National Prize 1998 (Cuba). She is the director (editor) of *Marx Ahora*, a Cuban theoretical journal and member of the International Council of the Historical-Critical Dictionary of Marxism, Hamburg, Germany. She is Director of the Julio A. Mella Institute of Philosophy.

John O'Neill

John O'Neill is Professor of Political Economy at the University of Manchester. He has written widely on philosophy, political economy and environmental policy. His books include *Markets, Deliberation and Environment* (2007), *The Market: Ethics, Knowledge and Politics* (1998) and *Ecology, Policy and Politics: Human Well-Being and the Natural World* (1993). He is co-author of *Environmental Values* (2008) with Alan Holland and Andrew Light. He has participated in a number of European and UK projects on environmental justice, climate change and biodiversity.

Vijay Prashad

Vijay Prashad is the Executive Director of Tricontinental: Institute for Social Research. He is the author or editor of several books, including *The Darker Nations: A Biography of the Short-Lived Third World* and *The Poorer Nations: A Possible History of the Global South*. His most recent book is *Red Star Over the Third World*. He writes regularly for *Frontline*, *The Hindu*, Alternet and BirGun. He is Chief Editor at LeftWord Books. Till recently, he was the George and Martha Kellner Chair in South Asian History and Professor of International Studies at Trinity College, Hartford, Connecticut. He was the Edward Said Chair at the American University in Beirut in 2013-14.

Sitaram Yechury

Sitaram Yechury is General Secretary of the Communist Party of India (Marxist). He joined the CPI (M) in 1975 and became the youngest member of the Party's Political Bureau in 1992. He was a Member of Parliament, Rajya Sabha, from 2005 to 2017. Sitaram has published extensively on issues of Marxist theory and has been active in formulations of CPI (M)'s policies and programmes, including, 'Hindu Rashtra', 'Socialism in the 21st Century' and 'Communalism versus Secularism'. For 20 years, he was editor of *People's Democracy*, the CPI (M) English-language weekly newspaper, and is the current editor of *The Marxist*, the theoretical quarterly magazine of the CPI (M).

OTHER PRAXIS PRESS TITLES

1000 DAYS OF REVOLUTION
Chilean Communists on the lessons of Popular Unity 1970-73
A fascinating account of the Allende Presidency, the dilemmas of peaceful and armed struggle for socialism, the role of US imperialism and domestic right-wing forces, and a self critical evaluation of the role of Chilean communists.

HARDBOILED ACTIVIST by Ken Fuller
The work and politics of writer Dashiell Hammett, crime fiction legend, communist and staunch opponent of McCarthyism. A critical review of his work and a definitive account of his political stand.

MEMOIRS OF A MILITANT by Kevin Halpin
Autobiography by one of the British labour movement's most beloved activists and a leading communist. A first-hand account of the great industrial struggles of modern times, written with enormous warmth and humour.

WHITE COLLAR, RED TIES by Steve Parsons (forthcoming)
A unique study of the Communist Party of Great Britain's activities among professional workers and intellectuals from its foundation until 1956. An essential contribution to the history of the British left.

For more details, contact praxispress@me.com

Lightning Source UK Ltd.
Milton Keynes UK
UKHW020342080319
338715UK00005B/76/P